31 DAYS FROM NOW

Sticking with "I DO" Overcoming "I'm DONE"

KENNETH KOON

Author of *Light of His Glory*

WESTBOW
PRESS®
A DIVISION OF THOMAS NELSON
& ZONDERVAN

WestBow Press books may be ordered through booksellers or by contacting:

WestBow Press
A Division of Thomas Nelson & Zondervan
1663 Liberty Drive
Bloomington, IN 47403
www.westbowpress.com
1 (866) 928-1240

ISBN: 978-1-5127-2441-7 (sc)
ISBN: 978-1-5127-2440-0 (hc)
ISBN: 978-1-5127-2439-4 (e)

Library of Congress Control Number: 2016900348

Print information available on the last page.

WestBow Press rev. date: 12/29/2015

To my beautiful wife, Sherry.
I am humbled by your love
and inspired by your wisdom.

Many women do noble things,
but you surpass them all.
—Proverbs 31:29

To four incredible men, my sons,
MaCrae, Nathan, Chad, and Tyler.
Through you I have come to better understand
my heavenly Father's love for me.

Children are a heritage from the Lord,
offspring a reward from him.
—Psalm 127:3–5

Contents

Foreword

From a Son

It was late at night when we pulled into the old country church graveyard in Wedowee, Alabama. We got out and stood in front of the tombstones, and for several minutes Dad spoke to me about the men now laid to rest. We imagined the lives they must have lived, the joys and the heartaches. Then Dad gave me a walking stick to keep the dogs at bay and told me to walk the three miles back to the lake house by myself. There was only the glimmer of a crescent moon to light my path down the lonely dark road. His final instructions were to stand in the graveyard till the truck was out of sight, and then I could begin my journey home.

Why would a dad do such a thing to his son? Some may think it was for punishment, but there was greater purpose in mind. You see, I had just celebrated my sixteenth birthday. My three older brothers had taken this same walk over the past seven years. I was the last son to take this journey. Being the youngest, I had not been invited on the walks of the other brothers. There was a certain level of secrecy associated with this experience. I knew my brothers had done what I was now doing, but that is all I knew, and now it was my turn. As the truck faded out of sight, I began walking.

Half a mile into the walk, I heard a voice call my name from out of the shadows. "Tyler Koon, your father sent me." It was my brother Chad, the next youngest. He joined me in the walk and shared with me experiences from his life that might help me in my journey too. Half a mile further, I heard another voice call my name. It was my brother Nathan. He too shared things that might help me in my journey. Then came my oldest brother, MaCrae, who shared with all his brothers truths he had learned on the journey. This went on as we walked, the voice from the shadows calling my name. We were joined in the journey by my uncle, Brian, and my dad's cousin, Merrill, each imparting wisdom from his life experiences that I was beginning to see would be of great benefit to me.

On the last leg of the journey, I heard the final voice coming toward me with great urgency. It was the voice of my father. He asked me what lessons I had learned along the way. He asked my oldest brother to pray a prayer over me. Then he shared many things with me, the last of which I will never forget. "The day will come when you find yourself standing in a graveyard once again, and I will no longer be with you. My greatest hope for you is not riches that this world has to offer, nor is it a life without struggles. My greatest hope is that in this life you surround yourself with those who will speak wisdom to you, that you allow them to walk with you. They are the ones whom the Father has sent to guide you in your journey. I bless you, my son. Your journey into manhood has begun."

We walked back to the house where Mom and all the ladies were waiting for a time of celebration. Dad presented me with two gifts— the first a beautiful sword known as the Sword of Solomon and the second a plaque with his personal blessing inscribed upon it. Both the sword and plaque are hung on my bedroom wall as a powerful reminder of a lifetime of love and wisdom.

That night was one of the most memorable nights of my childhood. I knew that I was blessed by my father in a way that perhaps many young men could only imagine. If you are one who never experienced such a relationship with your dad, allow me to introduce you to mine. He has a passion for reaching the hearts of men and seeing their lives transformed.

While my wedding "I do" is likely still a few years out, and I still have much to learn before I am ready for that day, I am thankful that I have already had practice in saying "I do" through the challenge Dad gave me that night. It is the same challenge that I make to you now to be an authentic man, a man of God who knows the importance of wisdom and pursues it as the most valued treasure to possess.

I am thankful that Dad has finally put his thoughts to paper. It is a reminder to me of all that he has sought to teach us boys throughout our lives, and it will be a blessing to me in the years to come just as I know it will be to you. I love you, Dad.

Tyler, son 4

The beginning of wisdom is this: Get wisdom.
Though it cost all you have, get understanding.
—Proverbs 4:7

Foreword

From a Friend

Probably the most far-reaching form of disciple making is the passage of wisdom and strength from father to son. After all, a man who is strong in character and mighty in spirit will be a blessing to his wife, children, and everyone around him. When a man is strong in the Lord, his family can find strength, and his church can be sturdy; society itself finds a foundation and direction. The failure of this passage means failure for society, the church, and the family.

As a young campus minister, about to have my first son, I went on a mission. A mission to talk to the fathers of my favorite male college students. A mission to find successful dads. Their sons were students who had sincere walks with the Lord and were "all men!" Young men who had a strength about them, not just physical but spiritual. One of those young men was Ken Koon. Yes, he was one of the strongest men physically at the college, but he had a sincerity and strength in his walk with Jesus that was undeniable. I talked with his father. I asked him about the most important thing he gave to his son. He mentioned several things, but it was all wrapped up in the response of "time." It takes time to raise up strong sons. God is not making any more of it—time, that is—so if it is important, then the time must be cleared to build a man. After all, it is the most important thing in the world … to fulfill the Great Commission and "make disciples" of our sons.

That young man, Ken Koon, now has raised four of his own sons. And we are allowed to watch and learn and laugh and cry through this book. It is a book of wisdom, with a foundation of truth from the Word of God, and in particular from Proverbs, and fleshed out in personal experience. Ken's journey may just help you to navigate life well and leave a legacy of blessing and strength.

Ken Jones, campus minister, North Georgia University

Preface

31 Days from Now started out not as a book but rather as short notes to my four sons. I was prompted by my oldest son's announcement of his engagement after witnessing another son's announcement of his "unengagement." After five years in a relationship (the last two engaged), this younger son finally said, "I'm *done!*" Thankfully he had not yet said, "I do." Yet in my counseling of soldiers and a few civilians over the years, I have worked with many married couples who have adamantly exclaimed, "I'm *done!*"

The reality is that *31 Days from Now* is not just a book for those engaged to be married. It is based on relationship principles found in the thirty-one chapters of the book of Proverbs, so it is applicable to any individual or couple no matter their age or how long they have been married.

These principles, when properly applied, are transformational. Whether you are preparing to soon say "I do" or you are one who is ready to throw in the towel by saying "I'm *done,*" I highly encourage you to consider the relationship principles found in Proverbs, the book of wisdom; however, you must also keep in mind that proverbs are not the same as promises. The book of Proverbs gives us wisdom in how to build relationships, but don't confuse them with promises. A soft answer doesn't always reduce the wrath of another person.

A child doesn't always return to the way he was raised. A godly mother doesn't always receive the praise of her children. Alternately, the promises of God are always true. If we confess our sins, God is faithful and forgives them. Those who hunger and thirst for righteousness will be filled. The merciful will be shown mercy. The pure in heart will see God. The peacemakers will be called children of God (Sermon on the Mount, Matthew 5).

As an individual or a couple, you can trust in the promises of God and apply the wisdom of God to firmly ground your relationship on God's truth. If *31 Days from Now* encourages you to develop this type of joyful relationship, then I have accomplished my purpose in writing it. Anything I have to say certainly does not add to what God has already said. I simply share with you a few nuggets and insights that I have gleaned and benefited from in my own marriage of twenty-nine years. I am still one who is learning and am humbled that you would walk with me in the journey.

In writing to my sons, my intention was to provide them with insights that they could consider individually and activities that they could work through with their fiancées. My hope is that you take a little time each day or each week to work through the activities and principles for the benefit of your relationship.

You will find discussion questions at the end of each chapter to work through with your partner. I encourage you to create both a couple and an individual journal to record your thoughts, because we have a tendency as human beings, especially we men, to forget the good when things are difficult. We all need reminding sometime. I have journaled since the age of fifteen and am thankful that I recorded my journey and reflected on it.

Even as I write these words, I am reminded of how blessed I have been throughout my marriage. It is my prayer that my sons and you experience a similar joy. By the way, today is the big day for my firstborn son.

Kenneth Koon, October 18, 2014

Acknowledgments

Thank you to all my Facebook friends who kept encouraging me to write a book after reading my posts and all the great folks at WestBow Press for your guidance in this publication.

Thank you to all the dear friends who contributed your anecdotes and nuggets of wisdom for chapter 24. Special thanks to Jim and Irene Murphy for a lifetime friendship of more than forty years. Sherry and I remember with great fondness visiting you guys in 1990 and the sweet time of devotion at the breakfast table. What an example of marriage as God intended!

Thank you to my sister, Leanne Farrington, for your editorial review. You have always been a Proverbs 31 woman. You and Brian are an example of a marriage built on wisdom, and it shows in how you have raised my three favorite nieces. Thanks to Deb Troxtel for your editorial review and your support and encouragement in the work of Armed Forces Mission (AFM).

Thank you to *all* the friends and supporters of Armed Forces Mission who made it possible to undertake this effort and to the AFM board of directors, who agreed that it was a worthwhile endeavor.

Thank you to my oldest son, MaCrae, and his bride, Lauren, for your encouragement to write the first chapter that you then willingly used in your premarital discussions. I was honored to officiate your beautiful wedding, and it was a tremendous joy to see how wisdom is already blessing your relationship.

Finally, thank you to Sherry, my beautiful bride, for all your love and support, and to my four sons, MaCrae, Nathan, Chad, and Tyler, who are (and always will be) my greatest motivation for seeking wisdom that will leave a legacy of honor.

Soli Deo gloria

Introduction

I had the incredible honor of becoming a father on June 17, 1990. A bundle of joy and energy in the form of 9.1 pounds of flesh and blood entered my life. It also happened to be Father's Day and the day my life was forever changed. Over the course of seven years, Sherry blessed me with three more sons.

After the first ten years, when the boys ranged in age from three to ten, I had the incredibly naive thought I might just write a parenting book. I wrote in my journal, *I got this...being a parent is a piece of cake.* After twenty-five years of being a dad though, I recently jotted some quick thoughts in my journal.

> *I'm glad I didn't write that book I thought I could write when they were three 'cause it's a different kind of strength I didn't know that I would need. They thought I was the strong one. That's what I led them to believe. But every night I'd thank the good Lord for what my boys were teaching me. It takes four boys to make a man by the grace of God and his helping hand. Wasn't me that was building boys, but it was boys that were building a man. I grew in faith, hope, and love, learned to trust when there're no answers,*

and after twenty years of raising sons, I thank God
for the boys that made this man.

Wow, I look at those words now. Someone with a bit of musical talent could almost have the workings of a country tune. The truth is being a father has been the song of my life, just as being married to their mother has been the dream of my life. That song plays even more sweetly in my mind as I look back with fond memories on the life we have had and the lessons I have learned along the way, both as a father and a husband.

Twenty-plus years seems like only yesterday. It was only yesterday we were putting train sets together under the Christmas tree, learning to ride a bike, playing T-ball, or riding the waves at the beach. It was only yesterday we were doing father-son campouts, learning to water-ski, and hitting the gym for the very first time. In spite of all the challenges and bumps along the way, these are the memories that stand out in my mind. These are the memories that are indeed very precious and sweet, and even now I am reminded that I still have much to learn about being a dad.

If being a dad has been a challenge, marriage has been something far beyond my ability to fully describe or explain, and thirty-one days hardly seems enough time for a father to help prepare a son for marriage. Again, I would be very naive to think that were even possible. That would be the equivalent of preparing a space shuttle for launch with a handful of bottle rockets. So it's not really new knowledge I hope to convey but rather a recap over the next thirty-one days of a lifetime of lessons learned along the way.

Sherry and I were married long before the advent of the Internet and all the dating and relationship websites. We didn't have the advantage of an algorithm to check our compatibility. What we did have, however, even after the second date, was a sense of the importance of establishing the budding relationship on solid ground. By the end of that first month, we had committed to sharing a prayer and devotional time each time we were together. I know … I get it. I may lose some men right here. You don't remember the last time you contemplated a spiritual thought, and you never prayed with a girlfriend. Maybe you have been married for a while, but you don't do so with your wife. Whatever your situation, you are reading these words now, so stay with me just a moment longer.

I don't have all the answers, and I still consider myself a student, but looking back on twenty-nine years of marriage I can say without hesitation that the strength of our marriage has been the spiritual dimension. That doesn't mean that I have gotten it right all the time. We haven't prayed together every day, and sometimes weeks go by without a concentrated focus on family devotions (more about that on day 25). I am prone like any man to letting the stuff of life get in the way. Lately though, as I have watched my boys grow into men, I have been keenly reminded of the need to get back to my own roots. In reading Proverbs again as if for the first time, I have gained new insights. In some areas, I have had to repent. I have been reminded that pursuing wisdom is not a "been there, done that" deal, but a daily process. So in many ways, no matter where you are in the journey, I am right there with you—still learning, still pursuing the love of my life as if for the very first time. It's good to know I'm not alone. Let's begin …

Couple Activity:

- Share your story with each other. What is your earliest memory? What inspired you? What was a challenge? What wisdom have you gained to this point?

Note to men: Whether you are one who is engaged to be married or you have been married for years, you still don't know her story. It's not about just knowing her favorite color or remembering her birthday or your anniversary. Her story is still unfolding. Pay attention if you plan to be part of it. Over the course of the next thirty-one days there will be increasingly challenging activities to pursue. It comes with growing in wisdom. For this reason, my encouragement is that you will work through the chapters in order. If you read the ending chapters first, you spoil the mystery of the things that wisdom calls you to do. Out of fear, you may put the book down and read no further. So start where you are, trust in the process, and discover what happens when you allow wisdom to come alive in your life.

Day 1

The Most Important Thing

Listen my Son.
—Proverbs 1:8

Whether you're preparing for the big day or you have been married for years, the most important thing is still the most important thing, and contrary to popular opinion and even my own, it's not your wedding day. Sure, it's a big day with many important things to do. It will doubtless be one of the most important days in your life. But all the traditional preparation—well, let me be straight from the start. The big day adds up to a big nothing and maybe even a lifetime of big pain and heartache when we don't understand the most important thing.

A myriad of details surrounds the wedding planning: venues to secure, guest lists to decide upon, social events to attend, caterers to call, music to select, and much more. All are vital activities in moving toward this very important day when the two of you say "I do." But none of them are the most important thing.

Recently Sherry and I were working with a young couple in premarital counseling. We knew in our hearts that it wasn't meant to happen;

we and many others were praying that this woman's eyes would be opened to see that this was not God's man for her. When she finally made the decision to break up with her fiancé, one of the young woman's concerns (and even hesitations to act) was related to all the money her parents had spent in preparation. To her relief, their response was, "Honey, that's not the most important thing." I knew that would be their response, just as it would be for any parents who understand the priorities of a godly life. Unfortunately some parents' actions prove that they indeed do not understand. One man we counseled received a text message from the woman's father after calling off his upcoming wedding. It read, "You do know we have purchased her dress. How could you do this?" Really? The reason to have a wedding is not because the dress was already purchased. Fortunately this young man was wise enough not to succumb to their berating.

Without doubt, the decision to marry is one of the most important decisions you will ever make. You are saying that above all others, this is the one person you want to be with in the good times and the bad. This is the one person who will know you like no other. This one decision will impact every other important decision that you make in life from this day forward—the number of children you will have, where you will live, the careers you will choose, and the friends you will make. All of these decisions and many more spring from the choice of a life partner.

Perhaps your wedding day is now a foggy memory, and you find yourself hard-pressed to recall the overwhelming joy of that occasion. You are not alone. Many of us men lose the wonder and awe that came with that new relationship. It's one of the reasons we wear rings on our fingers—to remind us of the love we found years ago and the commitment that we made to keep it alive forever. The preciousness of this one relationship with Sherry has served as a touchstone for recognizing the other important days in my life. In this vein, I will now share with you a letter that I wrote to my son, MaCrae, a few weeks before he married Lauren.

Dear Son,

From the time you could speak, your mother and I would ask you a question. It is the same question that I remind you of now. "What's the most important thing?" As a small child, you knew the answer we were looking for. Without fail, when the question was asked of you or your brothers, each of you would respond, "To be a man of God." Hopefully now, as a man, you have decided for yourself, and the answer is still the same.

I am reminded of Proverbs 1:8–9: "Listen, my son, to your father's instruction and do not forsake your mother's teaching. They are a garland to grace your head and a chain to adorn your neck." Of all the life lessons that we have tried to impart to you, we consider your decision to be a man of God to be most important. It is our prayer even now that you look to our Father as you make your decision to marry. We have prayed many prayers for you along the way and have even shed tears in those times when it seemed that you had lost sight of the most important thing. In those challenging periods, we reminded ourselves that you were not yet a man and continued to pray. We

3

also prayed from the day you were born that one day, you would meet a woman of God in search of a godly man for a husband.

As for myself, I must confess that I married way above my pay grade in this regard. Your mother's devotion to God has inspired me through the years to be more fervent in my own identity as a man of God. My prayer for you is that Lauren will do the same for you. May the two of you be incredible sources of encouragement and inspiration for each other. With a clear vision of what is truly most important, may you find strength for the challenges and joy in the journey. Finally, may you be to each other a reflection of God's love and grace in the years to come and throughout your life together.

Love, Dad

One of the greatest challenges for a man is in discovering his true identity. We think that our worth is all wrapped up in titles and accolades; however, when the façade of success or failure is laid aside, what is left? Who are you, really? You need to know. Your wife wants to know. Your marriage depends on the answer.

Many men today suffer from an identity crisis. We see it played out on a larger scale in our crisis of identity as a nation. We're not sure who is on our side anymore. We're not sure about our direction. If a man turns his eyes to the world, instead of our heavenly Father, for his identity, he will remain broken. He will be apt to pray wishful prayers, asking God to bless his ways when they are not God's ways.

Then he will wonder where God is in his life. "Where's God in my marriage?" he will ask.

The most important thing I want you to take away from our time together is a very clear and distinct picture of who you are as a man of God. It is my prayer that you will lay claim to your identity in Christ. When you know who you are in Christ, the relationship principles found in the book of wisdom will begin to make sense, and you will find a passion and purpose for your marriage that is truly transformational.

It won't be easy; it may not even be practical. All hell will break forth against you when you get in the game to have the marriage God intended you to have. God calls you to cling to the truth and apply the principles of wisdom, even when they don't make sense to you. In time, your understanding of God's way will grow, and you will be grateful that you were faithful in following His Word.

Couple Activity

- What does it look like to be a man or woman of God?
- What part does grace play in your personal identity?
- What are the important (immutable) truths on which to build your marriage?

Day 2

The Benefits of Wisdom

Turning your ear to wisdom and
applying your heart to understanding.
—Proverbs 2:2

School can give you a degree. An employer can give you a job, but the Lord can give you wisdom that opens up incredible doors of blessing. Wisdom is not the exclusive domain of the elderly. In fact, I have known many gray-haired men who seemed to lack wisdom. Encouraging a young couple to get married simply because the date has been set and the money has been spent demonstrates a lack of wisdom. Such an arrangement would most likely be doomed.

The Lord gives "knowledge and discretion to the young" (Proverbs 1:4) when they earnestly seek it like a treasure of great value. No marriage is immune to tough times. Life has a way of bringing grief our way without our help, but we do not need to bring grief upon ourselves. Wisdom brings with it the ability and potential power to help us decide responsibly. Using the knowledge that God so generously gives enables us to exercise discretion and thus avoid many of the pitfalls that newly married couples fall into.

When wisdom is applied to your marriage, it will store up success for you and help you understand how to do what is right in your relationship with your spouse. It will also protect you from others who do not have your best interest in mind, from the wayward woman to the person who is simply trying to do his job but without real benefit to you.

In our first week of marriage after returning from our honeymoon, we received a call from a door-to-door salesperson. She was selling encyclopedias; there was nothing wrong with them. I grew up with encyclopedias myself. What a great idea! For only nineteen dollars a month, these books could be ours for the kids one day. Thankfully a call from my dad just as we were about to sign up awakened me to the reality that we did not yet have kids, and by the time they were old enough to read, the books would be outdated. While I didn't call out for insight that day, I did get a call from insight that helped me to decide responsibly.

I was quick to listen to my dad then, but I have to confess I have not always been so quick to listen to my wife. That error is to my shame, for I have discovered over our lifetime together that she is truly a source of great wisdom. Her insights greatly benefit our marriage as well as my relationships with others. I have learned much about discretion from her over the years that would have been extremely beneficial in our early years of marriage had I been more attentive to Sherry's strength in this area from the beginning of our relationship.

"You're not my Holy Spirit" was one of the comebacks I would often give when Sherry was trying to provide input. She respected that comment. After all, who wants to claim they are the Holy Spirit? As I have matured spiritually, however, I have come to realize that the

Holy Spirit does work through others at times to help give direction to our lives. This observation is especially true in regard to your spouse—"and the two will become one flesh. So they are no longer two, but one flesh" (Mark 10:8).

A $200 juicer sits on our kitchen counter and has been used maybe a dozen times over the past few years. I thought that I had to have it. This machine was my solution for losing forty pounds. Sherry thought otherwise, and she was right. The fact is I really didn't bother to consult with her on the purchase. I did call her from the store as I was walking to the checkout line, but by that time my mind was already made up, and I wasn't willing to listen to what she had to say about the matter.

All of my life being married to Sherry, I have felt like I was living a beautiful dream. If any parts of it have been a nightmare, those parts are related to all the money I have wasted not using wisdom to make spending choices. Oh, that I would have awakened during those periods and discovered that wasting money was only a bad dream and I had actually been much wiser! We are all familiar with the jokes about women and credit cards; however, in our household having Sherry hold the cards was the right choice. I know that's not the case in every marriage; however, in a day where discretion seems to be passé and immediate gratification to be king for many men, the wise man has much to gain and a "good path" set before him that "will be pleasant to his soul" (Proverbs 2:9) when he realizes the benefits of tapping into the wisdom his wife has to offer.

Over the past few years, I have come to realize that Sherry really is my better half. Nowadays, I find myself bringing my thoughts and decisions to her, not because I need her to complete me as a man, but because I'm a better man with her. The simple fact of the matter is I make better decisions when I confer with her. God knew what He was doing when He said, "It is not good for the man to be alone. I will make a helper suitable for him." (Genesis 218) Perhaps you haven't noticed, but wisdom in Proverbs is referred to in the feminine. That reference is no accident. God knew what He was doing. Let's face it, we men need help, and I'm man enough to admit it!

The man fortunate enough to find a good wife has found a treasure. In His wisdom, God knew that leaving man alone would not be a good thing. Incredible blessing awaits the man who grasps this truth!

Couple Activity

- What will discretion look like within your marriage?
- What relationship wisdom speaks to you in Proverbs 2?
- How will you seek to increase wisdom as a husband/wife?
- What insights that the other may have right now will you be willing to attend to and apply in your life?

Day 3

Two Things Never to Leave Behind

Let love and faithfulness never leave you.
—Proverbs 3:3

In my first job after our wedding, I worked in the insurance and financial services field. It was 1986. I will never forget an interview with one young newly married couple. Their home was immaculate with the finest furnishings and entertainment. The Jet Ski was garaged next to a new BMW; the dog was professionally groomed. My first thought was that this couple had money to invest, which would result in a nice commission for me. I soon discovered though that they were living paycheck-to-paycheck, and their lifestyle was a façade. They didn't own the house; they didn't own the car; and they didn't even own the chair I was sitting in. They were $60,000 in debt with consumer credit, which in today's dollars would probably be close to double that figure.

Many newly married couples think they can have everything their parents have right from the start. Unfortunately in counseling couples over the years, I have found that disagreements over finances are somewhat common and can easily lead to separation and divorce.

I can't help but wonder how many of those men bought the same juicer I bought. When the Bible says, "a man will leave his father and mother and be united to his wife," the operative word is "leave." (Ephesians 5:31) Some things you just have to leave behind; you do well to be united with your wife in what those things are. One to consider is this idea of having it all *now*.

By the same token, two things must never be left behind: "Let love and faithfulness never leave you ..." (Proverbs 3:3). One way of demonstrating your love and faithfulness to your spouse is in the wise use of available resources. I will never forget how proud Sherry was that she had paid off her car before the wedding and entered marriage without debt. I will also never forget how foolish I was to pawn the title in an attempt to have start-up capital for a venture I never should have pursued. Good grief, it just hit me. It was an investment in a nutrition company. In the back of my mind, my thought was, "I'll be the poster boy for the company if I can just lose twenty pounds." Thankfully Sherry's love and faithfulness overlooked my indiscretion. She didn't hold it against me, but I did register a lesson learned in my thick skull—that is until I bought the juicer!

By demonstrating love and faithfulness to your wife in the area of finances, you will reap many benefits. Solomon goes on to say in Proverbs 3:4, "Then you will find favor and a good name in the sight of God and man." Your path will be straight, and you won't have to worry about bill collectors. When you shun the idea of immediate gratification and handle your finances with wisdom, you will be filled with more energy for those things in life that bring joy instead of heartache.

I was so proud of my youngest son, Tyler, recently. He was looking to purchase a used truck. This truck was a decked-out 4x4 with dual exhaust and a six-inch lift kit. He negotiated with the seller to within $500 of what he was willing to pay. When the man said he couldn't come down further, Tyler thanked him for his time and walked away. If I had only had that type of wisdom and restraint at his age, especially with all the weight loss gimmicks I have tried! Most interestingly, Solomon says, "This will bring health to your body and nourishment to your bones" (Proverbs 3:8).

Our spending choices can have a profound impact on our lives. Just this past evening, Sherry and I were having dinner with dear friends. They shared that their son is struggling financially due to a student loan of more than $100,000. Obviously education is a good thing, but that's a heavy burden for a young man. Such burdens that we bring onto ourselves often can cause us to question the benevolent hand of God.

Sometimes, a little thought regarding a purchase we want to make can prevent us from taking on an expense that will be particularly burdensome. For example, not long ago one of our sons asked if I would cosign for him to get a new "old" car. I told him, "No. Why would I do that? You have a car." It's an old Firebird that he paid cash for, but he is tired of sinking money into it for occasional repairs. Better an occasional repair bill than a car payment every month. I'm proud of him, too, by the way, for not pressing the issue. He knocked, but that door wasn't opening.

Many of the struggles in marriage that couples have are a direct result of extended financial obligations. Things get tight, and tempers get heightened. It's a slippery slope. We start wanting to blame others or think we are entitled. We get mad at ourselves, mad at others, and mad at God.

When I opened a real estate company in 1992, I did go to the bank to borrow start-up capital. I also borrowed money from my mother. I am grateful for her kindness, but both were obligations I wish I had never made. Our obligations were compounded when our oldest son was six years old and he fell off the top of a swing set, snapping his leg. He had to wear a full-body cast around his hips and both legs in order for the bone to heal properly. The medical bills put a severe crunch on our finances. I asked our church for help. I was very angry when they wouldn't agree to assist. "I'm a tither in this church, and you can't help me out? Just kick a dying horse why don't you?" Today I can honestly say that their "no" was the best thing that they ever did for me. When we are constantly depending on others, will we ever depend on God? My good friend, the gospel singer Dave Akin, sings, "Just when you think He's all you have, He's all that you need."

Financial miracles do happen, but one of the miracles that we often overlook is the wisdom God wants to impart. Wisdom looks for and finds better ways of doing things. At one point, our family had gone several years without a vacation. Either we didn't have time because I was selling real estate or teaching it to our agents, or we didn't have the money because it seemed every dime was going to running the company or paying bills. So I made the decision to expand the education division to train other agents. Then, for six years in a row, I took the whole family and even pastor friends on cruises that didn't cost me a dime. I did so by creating a program called "Cruising for Credit." Real estate agents signed up for some R&R and received six hours of continuing education credit for the classes we offered on board; I got many years of referral business as well. My only investment was six hours of my time. Maybe it's time for a marriage cruise …

God does orchestrate miracles, but sometimes miracles are simply wisdom in disguise. Either scenario is God at work. A very successful real estate friend bought a shopping center in Alabama that he thought could be revitalized. He made many changes with very attractive updates, but still things did not pick up. He began to sense that a liquor store in the shopping center was the cause of the sluggishness; however, he couldn't just kick the tenant out. They were properly licensed and had been located there before he had purchased the center. He waited out the lease and declined to renew it upon expiration. Within months, his shopping center gained more tenants, resulting in a positive cash flow. I have seen many couples experience similar turnarounds in their finances when they seek to honor God with what he has given them. Miracle or wisdom? Does it really matter? The blessing is the same.

Couple Activity

- What benefits can you imagine by exercising wisdom in regard to finances?
- What is your plan for paying off current debt?
- How will you seek to honor the Lord in your finances?

Day 4

Guard Your Heart

Above all else, guard your heart,
for everything you do flows from it.
—Proverbs 4:23

"I don't know why I did what I did." These were the words of a young man I was visiting in the county jail several years ago in my work with the Gideon organization. Proverbs 4:19 tells us, "But the way of the wicked is like deep darkness; they do not know what makes them stumble."

I have known others who didn't stumble into jail but stumbled in their marriage because somewhere along the way they failed to guard their heart. When you were a child, your parents had the responsibility of disciplining you and protecting you. In a very real sense, they were responsible for guarding your heart. Regardless of how well they did their job, now that you are an adult, it is your responsibility. As I write these words, I'm seeing much in the news about a young soldier who spent four years in the hands of the enemy because he walked away from his guard post. The consequences of not keeping guard can be devastating.

Maintaining your guard entails self-discipline in everything you do. The book of Proverbs speaks to this issue and gives credence to a theory that I have had for some time: There is ultimately no such thing as a lack of discipline. The one who does not possess self-discipline will eventually find it in the jailer, an enemy prison camp, the medical doctor delivering news on the steps needed to restore health, the bill collector, or the divorce court. We are all disciplined in one way or another. In such times, many people refuse to trust God because of all the bad stuff in their lives. It's the century's old question, "If God is so good, why do bad things happen?" Job was such a man. He had lost everything and thought he had the right to be the judge of God's goodness. He was wise in his own eyes, but he could not see with the eyes of God. Like Job, we would do well to heed the response God gives. "Would you discredit my justice? Would you condemn me to justify yourself?" (Job 40:8).

When our focus is on why God lets bad things happen to good people, we miss several important points. First, "good people" do not exist. God alone is good. I won't beat you up on this matter, nor will I expound on this subject here, since doing so is beyond the scope of this book. If you would like a reference, I suggest you start with one by a guy named John. The name of his book is John. Second, such statements are full of pride. Third, when we are full of pride, we are not walking in wisdom—at least not divine wisdom—and are engaging in foolishness. According to the apostle Paul, "For the foolishness of God is wiser than human wisdom, and the weakness of God is stronger than human strength" (1 Corinthians 1:25). As long as we depend on our own wisdom and strength, we will continually find ourselves against a wall, blaming God for the foolish situations in which we find ourselves.

First Peter 4:12 reads, "Dear friends, do not be surprised at the fiery ordeal that has come on you to test you, as though something strange were happening to you." The theologian A. W. Tozer wrote, "It is doubtful whether God can bless a man greatly until He has hurt him deeply." I know in my own experience that I have come to know God as sustainer, comforter, friend, and strength, because of those times when He was all I had.

Another important point of this fourth chapter of Proverbs is verse 24. We do well to keep corrupt talk far from our lips, whether it is our rants about the nature of God's goodness or the jokes we make about our spouses. Men, my encouragement to you is that you do well to never make your spouse the brunt of your jokes. The corresponding verbs to the adjective "corrupt" would be degrade, taint, warp, spoil, contaminate, harm, or damage. Such verbs also speak to the character of a man's heart. The man thinks he is being funny; others laugh; the woman smiles (and may even laugh along with the rest), but if the truth be known, it is a laugh of humiliation. If you look closely, you see no sparkle in her eyes.

A woman's countenance is often the best indicator of how well the man is doing at guarding his heart. By all means, a husband should laugh often with his wife but never at her expense. Guard your heart, and reap the reward of the sparkle in her eyes.

We'll look in greater detail tomorrow at maintaining your honor, but suffice it to say that you cannot do so when you fail to guard your heart. Proverbs speaks often to the issue of lust, as do other books of the Bible, to instruct us that it "brings death" and "war against your soul." It may not bring physical death, although that has happened to some, but it brings the death of relationship, peace, and the future

God intended. Yes, it is war—no less real than any played out on the battlefields of the world. The one who survives must be ever on guard and disciplined with his eyes, his words, and his thoughts. For the one who is willing to maintain this guard, incredible blessing awaits!

Couple Activity

- What acts of personal discipline will you incorporate for the benefit of your marriage?
- According to verse 4:7, how much is wisdom worth?
- What is meant by the words, "Give careful thought to the paths of your feet ..." (verse 4:26)?

Day 5

Maintain Your Honor

Drink water from your own cistern,
running water from your own well.
—Proverbs 5:15

With the engagement ring on her finger, you have fully declared your intention to live the rest of your life with the woman who has captured your heart. When the vows and wedding rings are exchanged, you will say before God and man, "This is the one with whom I am embarking on a great and lifelong adventure."

At that moment, your heart and mind will be filled with joyful anticipation of the journey ahead, but I would be remiss in my duties if I did not now warn you of the battle that also lies before you. The importance of guarding your heart (Proverbs 4) is the key to maintaining your honor (Proverbs 5). The fastest way to lose honor is through inappropriate relations with others.

I will never forget the looks of utter consternation I received from fellow classmates while participating in a small group discussion in a spiritual formations class in seminary. At twenty-three, I was the youngest man in the group, but something in me made me feel that all the pious talk in the group was a show. It didn't feel real. Finally, I couldn't take it anymore and blurted out, "If the truth be known, we are all a bunch of whoremongers in our thoughts, playing spiritual hopscotch, doing all we can to avoid the stone of lust that is clearly in our hearts and minds." Needless to say, I was shunned by the "super spiritual;" however, one man from the group caught up with me on campus the next day to say "thank you" and to acknowledge the same struggle in his own life.

I am reminded of the story of King David and Eleazar in 2 Samuel. When all the other men had fled, these two stuck together and defeated the enemy. Several years ago, I put together an accountability group using *Every Man's Battle* by Steve Arterburn and Fred Stoeker as our study guide. I remember the response of one man I invited to join us. "Nope, not interested. I'm accountable to God." I couldn't argue with that truth, but I couldn't help but wonder what he was trying to hide. Perhaps nothing, but in the battle for purity, a warrior who stands alone is easy prey. Unfortunately too many men flee from discussions of accountability and later find themselves wondering how they fell into the mire.

Proverbs 5 gives clear warning regarding the anguish that befalls those who are not prepared for the battle of sexual lust. A few moments of pleasure are not worth a lifetime of pain and regret, yet many end up there saying, "I don't know why I did what I did." The time to prepare for the attack is *now*, not in the moment of temptation. You maintain your honor and your new home by putting into practice today those things that will serve to guard your heart and your love. Continually keep before you the most important things and the things to never leave behind. The man who guards his heart and maintains his honor will avoid much pain and discover great joy.

Perhaps you have been married for some time and you have realized that marriage does not inoculate you against the spirit of lust. You will find great encouragement in the journey by surrounding yourself with other men who are in the battle, serious about standing strong against temptation and determined not to allow worldly pleasures to sway them from the path of godly marriage. I would highly encourage you to get a copy of *Every Man's Battle*. I have returned to it often over the years. The authors pull no punches in sharing their own stories and those of others who escaped the trap of sexual immorality; they remind husbands that "she's God's little ewe lamb ... and He has entrusted her to you ... Is there anything more noble than making a solemn promise to cherish your one and only?"

Job made a covenant with his eyes not to look lustfully at women other than his wife. Notice that Job did not say he wouldn't look, but that he wouldn't do so with lust. I would be extremely naïve if I said it is easy not to look and would be lying if I said I never do. Admiring beauty is not a sin, but when we do so without constraint, we are being naïve, or even intentionally sinful. We do well to follow Arterburn's lead and "bounce our eyes;" anything more is dangerous. We'll take a closer look at appropriate behavior in this area on day 28. Till then, remember that wisdom heeds the warning signs and reminds us that blessings are the reward for those who do so.

> May your fountain be blessed, and may
> you rejoice in the wife of your youth.
> —Proverbs 5:18

Couple Activity

- What boundaries are you putting in place in regard to others outside your marriage that will protect you and your relationship with your spouse?

Day 6

Practical Matters and a Reminder

Free yourself, like a gazelle from the hand of the hunter,
like a bird from the snare of the fowler.
—Proverbs 6:5

Recently a soldier shared with me his concern that he might lose his security clearance because he had cosigned a home loan agreement with a family member who had not been meeting the loan obligations. She had missed several payments, and the bank was contacting him with the past-due notices. Not only did this soldier have to pay several thousand dollars in mortgage payments, but he saw his credit rating suffer as well. As a soldier in a position that requires a high security clearance, he also risked losing his job.

Proverbs 6 warns us of the risk we take by becoming surety for another person. That's not to say that we shouldn't be charitable, but we should ensure that we can afford the help we are offering. In cosigning a loan for example, we must be able to cover the debt if the person we are helping does not make the required payments. It is one thing to make a mortgage payment for a friend or family member without ever expecting payback, but to secure the debt with your name is another matter altogether. Avoid it at all cost, or you may find yourself paying a cost you can't afford and can't avoid, like a bird caught in a snare.

Proverbs 6 also encourages us to work hard and save money for the future. Consider the ant. I am always amazed at the little line of creatures that seems to be moving with such purpose. Unlike the pesky housefly that is constantly flitting about, ants are on a mission. Each has a job to do and an organized means of doing its task. Interestingly the typical housefly lives fifteen to thirty days, while a worker ant can live up to seven years. In a laboratory setting, a queen ant has lived for more than twenty-five years. In the same way, you will set yourself up for the long-term by remaining organized in your finances. Begin a systematic plan of paying off the debt you have and saving money now. Don't delay in this matter. Your spouse will be glad, and your marriage will be blessed.

Proverbs 6 once again reminds us of matters we have already discussed. You can be certain that whenever a subject is repeated, you will be wise to take particular heed. So once again, we look at this matter of lust, specifically sexual lust, and not for the last time. Finances may seem like a practical matter, and lust may seem like more of a spiritual matter. The reality is, keeping finances in order does speak to spiritual matters, while avoiding sexual lust has very practical ramifications. Lust has destroyed many a man. It can destroy not only his finances but also his family. If the mission of protecting your finances is important, the goal of protecting your marriage is critical.

Obviously I have no statistics to back this next statement, but I can't help but believe that the application of wisdom in one area of life strengthens application in other areas of life, as well. In committing to apply the principles of wisdom to finances, you will obviously know that money is not to be devoted to charges for the topless bar or fees for the Playboy channel.

Creating a personal mission statement for your life and marriage is another very practical way to strengthen your marriage. It need not be long and complicated but should clearly set forth who you are, what you believe, and where you are headed. *Think* is a motto coined by Thomas Watson in 1911 that he later used to lead IBM. IBM's laptop computers are even called ThinkPads. We'll consider the *think* principle in another context in day 15, but for now consider that if one word can give guidance to a company, a mission statement can give guidance and direction to a marriage. The first time I met with the board of directors of Armed Forces Mission, I encouraged our team to adopt four simple words as our mission: "building resilience, restoring hope." In our second year of service, we experienced a 1,400 percent increase in our training participation. Keeping the mission in the forefront of our thoughts was a key. The King James Version of the Bible says, "Without a vision the people perish." Marriages do too.

Proverbs 6:22 alludes to the power of the guiding principles that evolve from a mission: "When you walk, they will guide you; when you sleep, they will watch over you; when you awake, they will speak to you." Once you have decided what that mission is, return to it often. It will be your touchstone when the battle rages.

When I was faced with some of the most difficult challenges of my life, it was my oldest son who reminded me that I am a soldier and to remember the Soldier's Creed: "I will always place the mission first.

I will never accept defeat. I will never quit. I will never leave a fallen comrade." When I was ready to give up on everything, including life itself, coming back to the mission for my life and marriage renewed my mind and my spirit and helped me to remember the source of my strength. So to my fellow comrades, I say, "Let's focus on the mission; don't quit; and never accept defeat." Victory is coming your way!

Couple Activity

- Begin thinking through your personal mission statement and your marriage mission statement. What would each of those include?

Day 7

Power in Its Purest Form

Bind them on your fingers;
write them on the tablet of your heart.
—Proverbs 7:3

Recently in the Sunshine State, a twenty-one-year-old man was arrested for soliciting sex from an undercover cop. Unfortunately such stories are not unusual, but this man was on his honeymoon. When he should have been celebrating his nuptials with his bride, he was out chasing other women. Hopefully most men would absolutely agree that this is the perfect example of a Proverbs 7:7 man. He had no sense about him. If we are honest, most men would also agree that sexual integrity is one of the greatest challenges we face.

Notice that I said "greatest challenges." One could argue that illicit sex is not man's greatest temptation. After all, the Bible makes no mention of a woman in the temptations Jesus faced in the desert. That's not to say that Jesus cannot empathize with our weaknesses. Hebrews 4:15 tells us that he does and, furthermore, that he was "one who has been tempted in every way, just as we are—yet he did not sin." The original downfall of man in the garden was not from sexual sin. Rather, in both the account of original sin in Genesis and the temptations of Jesus in the Gospels, the focus is on power.

Given the option, what would most men choose? A million dollars or a one-night stand with a beautiful woman? The answer may seem obvious—they would choose the money. In reality, while the lust for power in this world may seem greater than the lust for sex, every day men fall into affairs outside of marriage. As a result, what was once a beautiful relationship is marred, if not destroyed, and with a cost far greater than the man ever thought possible. Was it the lust for power or the lust for sex? Perhaps it was both.

Every man, even the simpleton, has a certain amount of personal power. He can use that power for good or evil. He can use it to build a happy home where love abounds or go in the "direction" of trouble according to Proverbs 7:8–9. When we operate in our own power, we have a strong tendency to corrupt that power. Money and sex are two of the most prominent symbols of power. Why do commercials push hamburgers with a voluptuous, scantily-clad female enticing us to join the "mile-high club"? It's because sex is power. Even fast-food restaurants know that truism, so they use it to increase their bottom line.

Wisdom increases a man's ability to act responsibly, which in turn increases his personal power. A simple man who, for lack of wisdom, loses his power is easily led astray by sexual temptation and caught in a noose that ultimately costs him much more than he wanted to pay. Sexual integrity is the proving ground for a life of integrity. Wisdom applied in this arena is a catalyst for a sound mind and a strong marriage. Responsibility in this regard trains the ear to hear wisdom's call in other areas of life as we have already discovered with our finances.

Wisdom in the use of power within marriage is vital. Power is neither good nor bad; unfortunately some men fail to exercise wisdom in their use of it. The "I'm the head of the house, so you will do what I say" attitude is one example of abusive power. In the military, insubordination, low morale, and even suicide have been attributed to the abuse of power by those in command in what is often referred to as a system of toxic leadership. Marriages can suffer from the same malady if power is exercised in an unhealthy way; however, the power God gives a man when he operates according to the principles of godly wisdom does not foster intimidation and fear within the marriage. In 2 Timothy 1:7 we read, "For the spirit that God gave us does not make us timid but gives us power, love, and self-discipline."

I have seen many men who claim to be operating in God-ordained power when they really aren't (I've been one). Some who use the Scripture to legitimize their personal power and authority over their spouse are often the greatest abusers of power. Margaret Thatcher said, "Power is like being a lady ... if you have to tell people you are, you aren't."

A particular form of power that a man should utilize in marriage is known as referent power. While Jesus operated in the power of the Holy Spirit, he related to others as a man with referent power, a power that was transformational. This power, unlike any other, instills loyalty, trust, and genuine respect. Ephesians 5:2 would be a good example: "Walk in the way of love, just as Christ loved us and gave himself up for us as a fragrant offering and sacrifice to God." If a man must insist on using the Scripture to define his power, he should first reference and become thoroughly familiar with every instance of the word "love." Then he should act upon every command and idea of how to best implement love toward his wife without ever quoting a verse to her about how she should respect him and love him the same way. This is power displayed in its purest form. That's the power Jesus displayed at the cross. When you can fully love your wife the way Christ loved the church, then maybe, just maybe, you have earned the right to tell her how she should love you. Till then, get your marker out, and start highlighting.

Couple Activity

- What does personal power mean to you?
- How does wisdom increase personal power?
- How will you use your personal power to build and strengthen each other?

Day 8

Game-Winning Run

Does not wisdom call out?
—Proverbs 8:1

As an avid fitness enthusiast, I was very excited about my first job interview after graduating from college. I had applied for an assistant manager position at a large fitness club in Atlanta. As I continued to listen to the potential employer, however, I did not so much hear his voice as I heard an inaudible one that spoke to my heart—"*Stop … this is not for you.*" The interview went well, but as I walked out the door, again the voice sounded even louder—"*Stay out!*" Watching the six o'clock news that evening, I was amazed to see the man with whom I had interviewed and two employees in handcuffs being placed in a police car. They had been arrested for credit card fraud. That evening in my devotional time I read from Oswald Chambers: "Doubt is not always a sign that a man is wrong; it may be a sign that he is thinking."

Wisdom called out to me that day. The signs were clear. I'm glad I was paying attention. What amazes me more nowadays is not so much that wisdom calls out but rather that I still fail to see the signs or read the signals that Sherry gives me at times. One of the great antidotes for my stubborn rebellion over the years is to return often to the book of Proverbs and other books like *My Utmost for His Highest* by Chambers and *Every Man's Battle* by Arterburn.

"At the highest points along the way, where the paths meet, she (wisdom) takes her stand." (Proverbs 8:2) At those crossroads of life, wisdom will guide the person who seeks it. That observation does not imply that life will always be easy. Sometimes it feels like the bottom of the ninth, and we're trailing by two with two outs. If we rely on faith and wisdom, however, we gain a rich inheritance of honor and sound judgment which ultimately is of greater value than anything we might acquire without it. Worldly riches can quickly fade away, yet faith and wisdom are an "enduring wealth" not dependent upon circumstances.

Faith and wisdom work hand-in-hand. Again, Chambers says, "Faith is deliberate confidence in the character of God whose ways you may not understand at the time." We will be called many times in life to exercise faith. True faith is never blind faith, as the skeptics would say. The true danger in this situation is not so much that we cannot see the signs but that we will not believe that God gives wisdom to those who seek it.

Through faith and wisdom we stay in the game. The one who is wise increases in wisdom. He seeks after it as a great treasure with the faithful assurance that in seeking he will find it. A game is there for the winning; in that game, you and your wife are on the same team.

In the past few years, I have recognized that many times in my life I have sought the counsel of others without considering the incredible wisdom that is available to me in my wife. Many times I have sat with her to share a "new insight" I had gained from visiting with a friend. In the early years she would remind me that she had recently told me the very same thing but that I wasn't listening.

Guys, listening in any setting is a key to wisdom; furthermore, listening to your wife is a key to great joy and blessing for your marriage. I cannot even begin to imagine how hurtful it was for Sherry that I could hear what others were saying but not what she wanted to communicate. Nowadays she doesn't do much reminding, because she too is growing in wisdom, but also because I have realized that she is my senior counsel when I need the insight of another person.

Sherry is not only my senior counsel; she's also a great coach. Most wives are if we men pay attention. I don't want to toot my own horn, but I think I've gotten better with age at reading the signals Sherry sends my way, but I still miss them if I'm not paying attention. I enjoy watching professional coaches swiping their arms and touching their ear, their cap, and their belt buckle in rapid succession as they signal a bunt or a go-ahead run. I'll admit I'm not that good. For me it's more little-league speed. Nice and slow, coach.

To this day, when I am speaking in public and Sherry is in the audience, I know I need to wrap up when she touches her right ear. When she touches her brow, I need to move to the next point. Most times I read the signals correctly, but sometimes I don't. Marriage is that way. We don't get it right all the time. Sometimes you're just not sure what the signal is, but if your attitude is one that believes you're both in this game to win, then you don't let defeat enter your mind.

A great illustration of how this confidence works was seen in the seventh game of the 1992 NLCS, the Braves vs. Pirates. The play still stands out as one of my all-time favorite moments in Braves baseball. The Pirates' pitcher, Doug Drabek, had shut the Braves out for eight innings. The game was at the bottom of the ninth with two outs. Dave Justice was on third; Sid Bream, the winning run, was on second. Francisco Cabrera cracked a line drive to left; Justice scored; and Sid Bream rounded third, sliding into home inches from the ball thrown by Barry Bonds to win the NLCS and head to the World Series. Bream later said, "A lot of people asked me over the years, 'Why didn't you stop when (third-base coach) Jimmy Williams gave you the stop sign?' To this day I don't know if he gave me the stop or not." It was an amazing win, especially given that Bream, with five knee surgeries under his belt, was not that fast, according to his own admission.

As husbands, none of us are "that fast," so we sometimes miss the coach's signals. Proverbs 8:1 raises the question, "Does not wisdom call out?" It's not a call to perfection or to read every signal accurately. It's a call to stay in the game when you're trailing in the bottom of the ninth.

That winning run opened incredible doors for Sid Bream. He would be the first to tell you that had he not been the man that scored that run, he would have retired a few years later and faded into the history books as just another player. He tells folks now that as he stood on second, he was thinking, "This team has had a never-say-die attitude all year long. We've come from behind before. We can do it again." When he took his lead off second, he was thinking that on contact he was going all the way, and the rest, as they say, is history.

I almost envy newly married men who are just getting started in the marriage league and already have a firm grasp of the importance of reading the signals. For me and many of my friends, it has taken longer; we have missed the signals so many times. Thankfully some of us have that "never-say-die attitude." Slowly but surely, we are learning that one of the greatest ways to demonstrate wisdom in our own lives is to tap into the wisdom that God makes available to us through our wives.

Maybe you have spent years missing the signals your wife sends your way. Stop beating yourself up over all the missed signals. Wisdom never calls you out to beat you up but rather to build you up. You've got a game to win, even if you are down by two runs.

When the history of your life is recorded, what will the story tell? Will it be one of overcoming power displayed in the life of a man who believed even when he was down? Will it be one that your fans will share with fond recollection and inspiration? Oh, you think you don't have fans? They're there all right—your wife, your children, one day perhaps your grandchildren, the guys at the office, the neighbor who's limping worse than you. They may be a bit excited to see you standing on second base, with limited chances but great hope, to pull a play off. If you'll step off that base, then, and take the lead, you might just be surprised to see your fans cheering you on. The game-winning run is rounding third if you have faith enough to believe.

Couple Activity

- How would she feel knowing she is your primary "go-to" person for insight and decisions?
- In what areas of your life will you begin to implement that commitment now?
- Make sure you have the signals right. Ask her to coach you through them. She'll be glad to; that's what great coaches do.

Day 9

Invitations

She has sent out her servants, and
she calls from the highest point of the city.
—Proverbs 9:3

Recently I found myself with a major scheduling conflict. I was scheduled to speak in Jackson, Mississippi on the very day that I was to be teaching in Fort Dix, New Jersey. Both events were important, yet I had to make a decision. Neither choice seemed obviously better. Proverbs 9 describes two invitations that would seem to be much more obvious.

The first invitation is from Wisdom. She has prepared her house for a grand occasion. She has selected the finest meat and wine and has sent her servants to personally deliver the invitation. The second invitation is from Folly: "She is simple and knows nothing." She too calls out from the highest point in the city. She has prepared her house with stolen goods that must be consumed in secret. Wisdom's invitation is to "leave your simple ways … and walk in the way of insight." Folly's invitation is to remain as you are, for she has nothing to teach you, since she knows nothing herself. So which invitation do you accept?

As you prepare invitations for your wedding day, I strongly encourage you to consider what it is you are inviting people to attend. Certainly it is a celebration and a time filled with laughter and joy. It is truly your very special day. As Kool and the Gang might sing, it's "a celebration to last throughout the years." Why don't you stop to think how it might also be an occasion for those in attendance to see wisdom displayed and to gain insight that perhaps they have never considered before?

As you establish your home, what invitations will you extend to others who might enter it? Will it be a home where wisdom or folly is the honored guest? Wisdom opens doors for incredible blessings to flow into your home. As you entertain others, those who are wise will be "wiser still." Your home will be a refuge for those who are hurting and need a word of encouragement. You will be a conduit through which God blesses those in need. Within this process, you will reap great benefit: "If you are wise, your wisdom will reward you ..." (Proverbs 9:12).

Maybe you have been married for a while. Have the invitations you have accepted or extended to others resulted in the expansion of wisdom or folly? For example, what do you do when you and your wife experience a challenge in your marriage? When a man is struggling in his relationship with his wife and begins to console himself by sharing those struggles with a female coworker or other acquaintance, the warning bells should be sounding with great alarm. I would put such activity in the category of folly, a place of "stolen goods consumed in secret." I once had a man tell me, "What my wife doesn't know won't hurt her." The fact is that it already has. Such a situation is akin to undetected cancer that will eventually manifest itself.

Shortly after I had interviewed a woman for a position with our company, she started sending me e-mails asking me to have lunch so that we could discuss her upcoming real estate test. I declined and suggested that she study. Her advances became even more aggressive. I joked with one of my Sunday school members who had an office across the hall, "I think the devil is after me; after all, she was wearing a blue dress." In her last e-mail, she told me her husband would be out of town the next weekend and actually went into detail on what we could do. What she didn't know was that I had passed every single e-mail along to Sherry. I responded to her last e-mail by demanding that she remove my name from her contacts and make no more attempts to contact me. I signed it Ken and Sherry.

Any ability I had to overcome that situation had nothing to do with me. In fact, it frightens me to think that I was even flattered. Frighteningly that's the nature of the flesh, and to the flesh, "stolen water is sweet; food eaten in secret is delicious!" No, I can't take credit for saving myself from the "realm of the dead" as Solomon describes it. My strength to resist all came from the grace of God. His grace was sufficient. As men, we must recognize that we need His salvation in this area in the very same way that we need salvation for our souls. The amount of love I have for my wife or she for me is not the pertinent issue here. Paul told Timothy, "I am convinced that he is able to guard what I have entrusted to him." (2 Timothy 1:12) Regarding our faithfulness to our wives, we must trust God. Yes, He tells us to guard our hearts, but I need someone guarding me as I guard it. At least my wisdom is telling me so. God's strength, not my own, is the key factor. Through the wisdom He gives, we are able to discern the invitations we give and receive.

If you struggle to know how to communicate about issues such as these with your wife, hold on. We'll be covering such strategies in further detail soon. Until then, give some thought and discussion to the following questions.

Couple Activity

- In what ways will you seek to display wisdom as you entertain others in your home?
- Describe a time when you were able to be a source of wisdom and encouragement to someone.
- What safeguards will you employ to guard against giving and receiving unwise invitations?

Day 10

About the Dishes

Lazy hands make for poverty,
but diligent hands bring wealth.
—Proverbs 10:4

The Swiss psychologist, Carl Jung, coined the phrase "synchronicity" in the 1920s to describe the occurrence of two or more events that appear to be meaningfully related but not in a cause/effect manner. It's the idea of two or more unrelated events that seem to have some type of meaningful purpose. Perhaps one of the best examples in Scripture is the story of Joseph, of the Old Testament. He was thrown into a pit by his jealous brothers, sold into slavery, and jailed. He interpreted dreams, including dreams of a fellow prisoner and a king, and ended up second in command of Egypt. These seemingly unrelated events culminated in Joseph saving his family from famine years later, and these events also allowed the growth of Israel out of this family. While some might argue causality, we really cannot say; however, what we can see is that various parts did come together to make an interesting whole. Often little things in life add up to make a *big* difference.

Recently, as I was waiting to take a flight to Dallas, I spoke by phone with a family member who had called off her wedding. As I walked down the Jetway to board the plane, I texted her that God's grace would sustain her. Once I was seated on the plane, a man who appeared rather distraught sat down next to me. As I engaged him in conversation, I discovered that he was fifty years old and had been in Atlanta visiting his girlfriend. Earlier in their relationship, they had been discussing the possibility of marriage, but now she was not willing, because he did not believe in God. For the next one and a half hours on the plane, we talked about the grace of God. Before we landed in Dallas, the man had accepted the gift of God's grace. A situation of synchronicity had unfolded, resulting in a transformed life and affirming once again in my own heart and mind that I, too, am totally dependent upon the grace of God. I returned home a few days later with a strong desire to show more grace in my own marriage.

On first look, chapter 10 of Proverbs might appear to the reader to be a series of unrelated sayings; however, when taken together the parts make a coherent whole. Diligent hands … wise lips … a heart that fears the Lord—in one regard they stand alone, and yet, together they bring blessings of the fruit of wisdom and favor.

On a practical level, making the bed, putting down the toilet seat, taking out the garbage, and putting away the dishes after a meal may seem to be unrelated events. One does not cause the other, yet they are related by meaning within a shared household. Add to these tasks time in prayer together, kind words, and affectionate touches. These activities are just a few of the building blocks to a strong marriage—a starting point, a demonstration of wisdom, and a foundation for the relationship to grow. Such an environment is a place where love abounds.

Speaking of the dishes … it's not her job. Truth be known, she doesn't owe you a meal either. I cringe to think of all the times I have walked away after a good meal leaving dirty dishes on the table. Over time, I improved my behavior, but when I first did so, I was looking for praise from Sherry for my help in the kitchen. Why do we men behave this way? We do something we should do anyway and then think we've garnered some kind of epic achievement that will cause our wives to worship us as if we had just slain a dragon.

One more thing: How many times have you thought your wife is just too wrapped up in her feelings? We claim that men aren't into that "touchy-feely stuff." The truth is that we are, but in a different sort of way. A woman's feelings are generally somehow directly connected to relationships, whereas a man's feelings are generally focused on the activities he likes and dislikes. If we start doing the things we don't feel like doing, we might just find that our feelings change. We would begin to see the positive impacts over time in both practical and emotional ways. Honestly, in counseling many couples over the years, I have witnessed far more emotion-based men than I have women and far more logical and rational women than I have men.

We men are not without hope. We started today's devotion looking at the importance of diligent work. Many a man has applied this principle to build financial empires or progress upward in corporate settings in order to achieve financial success. Let's apply this same principle within our marriages and see what we can build. Start with the dishes in the kitchen sink.

Couple Activity

- Share with each other something that the other has done that conveys love and meaning for you.
- Tell your spouse of at least one activity or task the other could engage in on a regular basis that you believe would benefit your home and/or relationship.

Day 11

Look for the Good

Whoever seeks good finds favor.
—Proverbs 11:27

I recall a story I heard as a child about a wise old man who sat outside the general store of a little country town. A newcomer to the town walked up to him and said, "I'm new to this here town. Can you tell me what it is like to live here?"

The old man responded, "What was the place like that you came from?"

"Well it was horrible. People were out for themselves; it was not easy to make friends; and I couldn't wait to get out of there," said the new resident.

To which the old man responded, "Well, I think you will find this to be a similar kind of place."

The next day another newcomer walked up and asked the old man the same question. Again, the old man responded by asking the newcomer about the town from which he had come. The newcomer said, "Well it was a wonderful place. The people were so kind. Most folks there would give the shirt off their back to help out folks in need."

To which the old man responded, "Well, I think you will find this to be a similar kind of place."

Many years before cell phones, I had asked Sherry to pick me up at the airport. She couldn't find me, so not knowing what to do she went back home. I called and, with a very unkind tone, told her to come pick me up. When she arrived, I gave her a few more choice words. I was a total idiot in the situation. Although over twenty-five years ago, I still remember how the interchange crushed her spirit. Had I been looking for the good, I would have found favor from my wife and perhaps even a welcome home kiss. A few years later, with the advent of cell phones, I had an expectation that she would answer the phone immediately whenever I called. Again, I was a total idiot.

Early in my marriage, I did not understand the power of looking for the good. Nowadays when I get Sherry's voice mail instead of her live voice on the phone, my first thought is that Sherry must be busy and unable to answer at the moment. I think fondly that she may be talking with another family member or counseling a friend. I will leave her a short message and look forward to talking with her when she has free time.

When it's ten at night and she wants to know what I am doing in the kitchen or she gives me that look, letting me know I've had enough to eat when we are dining with friends, I know that she is only trying to help and must want me to stick around. When Sherry tells me not to wear those "old-man socks" with my shorts, I realize that she is not nitpicking but rather that she just wants me to look good. I appreciate the help! In this area too, I married way above my pay grade.

In addition to Sherry's strong devotion to God and her beauty, I so appreciate her wisdom and willingness to apply it. Though I may hold three degrees, Sherry's ability to tap into her vast reservoirs of wisdom is far more advanced than mine. Thankfully I have learned and continue to learn that it is in my best interest to run things by her—whether it is a purchase I want to make or the way I plan to say something when I am speaking in public. I've learned that my most valuable key to being a public speaker is making use of Sherry's input in my preparation. Even in writing this book, I have made many revisions based on her ideas and thoughtful feedback.

In those rare occasions when I think Sherry should have done something in a different way or I am sharply hurt by something she has said, the best thing I can do is *look for the good.* This practice has been a great blessing for me. I wish I had learned it earlier. Sherry is never trying to harm me. She truly does have my best interest in mind, because my best interest is our best interest.

In this respect and many others, I am so thankful that our boys have taken after their mother. I have always tried to maintain a positive attitude about the things that comprise my life (for example, running my business affairs, writing sermons or speeches, taking a physical-abilities test as part of my military training). Sherry does the same, but she is much better than I am at maintaining a positive attitude about people. One day at baseball practice, when Nathan was about twelve, the coach had the guys running laps around the bases. The coach's son was starting pitcher, although the only thing he was really good at was acting like a small child when Nathan pitched. While the other boys were running, the coach's son was standing near the baseline, not being made to join the group. As Nathan ran past him, the boy stuck his foot out and tripped Nathan. I was honestly hoping Nathan would get up and deck him. Instead, Nathan got up, dusted himself off, and kept running. Yep, I am glad my boys take after their mama!

At times, you may struggle to see the good in your marriage. Even now, you may be entrenched in such a challenging time in your relationship. You have the ability to find the good; you just need to practice. It's time to run some laps. Perhaps instead of being mired in the negative, you are a man who can see a showroom classic under the rust of a worn-out jalopy or the value and character in a ratty rental property that will someday return far more than you invest. If this description fits you, then you already know how to look for the good.

Granted, women aren't cars or rental houses, but the man who is willing to apply as much time and effort to his marriage as he does to other pursuits will be richly blessed. By looking for the good, you can help restore the classic beauty and value of a relationship that may have been marred by years of neglect.

Couple Activity

- Express your commitment to each other that you will endeavor to always look for the good.
- What is one good thing about your partner for which you are, right now, thankful?

Day 12

The Power of Words

The words of the reckless pierce like swords,
but the tongue of the wise brings healing.
—Proverbs 12:18

In chapter 12 of Proverbs, we note the many individual pieces of advice that yet have a common theme woven through them. As in the overall book of Proverbs, this chapter highlights the great importance of our words and actions. Every relationship in life is either established or destroyed by the things we say and do.

Your words and actions are so critical for establishing a loving and godly foundation for both your home and your relationship with your bride. Being ever mindful of developing and using the wisdom we have discussed in earlier chapters to speak and act in loving and thoughtful ways is a key to a happy marriage. In turn, your behavior will foster your wife's love and respect and encourage her to stay on course with you in applying God's best for your marriage and the course of your lives.

Proverbs 12:4 tells us, "A wife of noble character is her husband's crown." One of your responsibilities is to treat her as such. No man should act recklessly with a crown of jewels, for if he does, he proves himself unworthy of the treasure with which he has been entrusted.

Unfortunately, after many years of counseling both soldiers and civilians, I have encountered some men who seem just to be looking for opportune times to strike their wives with hateful words. Such a man fails to see that he himself is his own worst enemy, not his wife. Of course, I have encountered a few women, too, who at times also act in ways that crush their husbands. Proverbs 12:6 states, "The words of the wicked lie in wait for blood, but the speech of the upright rescues them." When tensions are high, as they are apt to be at times, you must decide what course of action you will take with the words you speak. Will you be a rescuer or a terrorist to the one you promised to love and cherish?

When the difficult discussions do come, remember you do well to hear her out. Stop looking for words to defend your position or actions. Remember—"the way of fools always seems right to them, but the wise listen to advice" (Proverbs 12:15). I look back now with great regret that I did not learn this truth earlier in my marriage and even in my interactions with others. Even now, I recall a conflict that I had with someone where, like a fool I showed my annoyance at once, not realizing that the prudent (the wise) course was to overlook an insult. Sherry had advised me with godly wisdom not to react rashly; if only I had slowed down to heed her advice. My prayer is that I continue to dedicate the time and attention that God advises to listening closely to and applying Sherry's and other Christians' advice to the inevitable challenges of life.

If you are just now embarking on this journey of marriage, you are no doubt anticipating a life filled with good things. The starting point of your journey with your wife is based on your words and actions: "From the fruit of their lips people are filled with good things, and the work of their hands brings them reward" (Proverbs 12:14).

If you have been married for a while, you no doubt recall those times when your words were reckless; you may even have a pattern of speaking in a thoughtless and impulsive manner. In either case, you can reframe the way you respond to stresses and challenges so that your words do not inflame an already difficult situation. In the past, when you spoke recklessly, you weren't fighting *with* your wife; you were fighting *against* her. For you and your wife to win in the game of marriage, you must recognize that you are on the same team. You must work together in the fight *for* your marriage.

When you see that you are heading into one of those inevitable disagreements with your wife, immediately focus on keeping your words and actions toward a mutually respectful and wise resolution. You can think back to advice from the referee in the *Rocky* movie for an analogy on "fair fighting" with your wife. For example, he directed the fighters to make "clean breaks"; retreat to a neutral corner in the event of a knockdown (or, in your case, a barrage of angry and tense words); and to engage in a good, clean fight. If Rocky and Apollo could fight fairly, certainly you can do an even better job when in challenging discussions with your wife. Fighting for marriage is a fight that will reap great rewards for both husband and wife.

Fighting for is a completely different mind-set from fighting against. When my dad, at the age of forty-four, was told he had inoperable cancer and was given at best three years to live, he began a fight for life. He didn't focus on the cancer that was fighting against him. He was focused on what he wanted. He wanted life, not cancer. He wanted to see his two children grow up and marry. He continued to work hard in his business until the last two weeks of his life, even though there were days when the chemo had zapped nearly every ounce of his physical strength. At night, he would come home and watch *The Andy Griffith Show* and laugh at Barney's antics. He visited others who had cancer, encouraging them to fight for life. He was a man who practiced looking for the good in everything. When he finally passed nine years later, many people told me that they did not even realize Dad had cancer, simply because cancer was not his focus. One man particularly stands out. I asked him how he knew my dad. He said, "I pumped his gas." I also discovered that this man had cancer. Dad bought his gas from the only full-service station in town and paid more for it, just to share a word of encouragement with someone who needed it. By the way, eleven months after walking my younger sister down the aisle, Dad finished his fight and received his reward.

We all know people who just seem to fall into trouble as soon as they open their mouths. Several years ago, I had the task of serving as jury foreman in a nasty divorce case involving a very wealthy couple. In my opinion, the husband gave a whole new meaning to the definition of scum. Interestingly enough, the women of the jury were far more lenient on the husband than the men were. Looking back now, I can't help but wonder if their tolerance was due to their low expectations of men. After much discussion, we came to a decision that left me heartbroken for his wife. I was also encouraged, however, by some of the other men on the jury, who expressed that they wanted to see men live by a godlier standard than the husband did in this case. I'm pleased to know that many more of us are out there! Wisdom teaches us to live by a higher standard and is demonstrated in the words we speak. Be encouraged!

As you consider today's couple activity, keep a few ground rules in mind. When one of you is speaking, the other should be *listening*! One of the props that has helped Sherry and me, as well as other couples, is a "talking stone" or other object. Whoever has the talking stone is the one talking. Keep in mind the activities you have already worked through. Consider them the building blocks to today's activity. Your identity as a man or woman of God allows grace to work through you now. Because of your identity, wisdom that honors God is flowing through you and your partner. You have a mission that is continually moving you closer to your true identity. Your personal power is motivated by a love that builds and strengthens each other. You are a source of wisdom and encouragement to each other. In sharing truths between yourselves now, you are committing to one another to endeavor to always look for the good. Finally, one more thing: promise not to throw the stone at each other.

Couple Activity

Today's activity will be a challenge. Don't let it become a fight.

- Listen as she tells you about a time when your words felt more like a sword than love.
- How does wisdom guide your response?
- Listen as he tells you about a time when your words felt more like a sword than love.
- How does wisdom guide your response?

Day 13

The Illusion of Success

One person pretends to be rich, yet has nothing;
another pretends to be poor, yet has great wealth.
—Proverbs 13:7

When the boys were little, Christmas around our home was more about being together than anything else. We exchanged a few gifts, but we didn't incur great financial obligation to do so. We laughed when some friends told us their children had prayed, "God, thank you that we are not like the Koon boys." Sadly though, years later this couple and many others like them struggled in their marriage, often directly due to an overextension of credit.

Pretending to be rich is a path that has destroyed many marriages. Buying things on credit creates the illusion of success, but the success comes with a heavy price. Proverbs 13:10 is particularly applicable here: "Where there is strife, there is pride ..." Pride leads us to pretend that we are something we are not. Pride and its accompanying pretense is at the root of the strife. The spending, the extended credit, and the stuff we surround ourselves with is simply the symptom. Left unchecked, such a cycle may ultimately leave us with almost nothing.

The credit card companies love to show all the exotic places you can go and the things you can have; some even offer cash back. Such an offer seems like an incredible deal. With that thinking, I could convince myself that if I had just had the right card when I bought that juicer, I would be so much happier now. The similarity to the Garden of Eden is uncanny. With this card, you have the freedom to achieve your desires without limits; you can have the power of God. This thinking just leaves out the realization that you will also bring evil upon yourself. The companies never show a couple paying the bills laden with interest, getting the collection calls, or sitting in bankruptcy court.

One of the immediate challenges and temptations for a newly married couple will come when friends begin to surround themselves with the illusion of success. Having nice things is not the problem per se, but if you are spending next week's grocery money on this week's plasma TV or video game, then your life is sorely out of balance. Proverbs 13:11 says, "Dishonest money dwindles away, but whoever gathers money little by little makes it grow." When we are constantly spending future income on current wants, we greatly diminish (if not obliterate) our ability to truly save for the future. In a way, we are being dishonest with ourselves. We are never able to enjoy the benefits of compound interest or a good return on investments when all available resources are used to maintain the illusion.

I'm convinced that we must learn humility in the use of our money; otherwise, we may be financially humiliated. Humbling ourselves is often a painful process. In my last three years of high school, my parents sacrificed to put my sister and me in a very affluent private school. The student parking lot was filled with the latest TransAms, BMWs, Jaguars, and the like. My car was a 1963 VW my dad had purchased the year I was born. I drove it for a year until the night I snuck out of Sunday worship and rolled it over doing donuts in the church parking lot. I then bought a 1963 Olds Dynamic 88 for $300 plus the scrapped VW. This car was so ugly that every day my sister made me drop her off a block from school. I'll admit it was one unsightly jalopy.

You are probably aware of the traditions surrounding anniversary gifts—the first year is paper; the twenty-fifth is gold; and the sixtieth is diamonds, for example. Sherry bought me a diamond cluster ring that I wanted for our tenth anniversary, even though we couldn't really afford it. "Let's just go all out," I had said. Not long after, I was having lunch with an uncle and whining about my finances. He couldn't help but take notice of the big gold and diamond ring on my right hand. To this day, I struggle to wear that ring and keep it, since it is a reminder of how easy it is to give in to the desire for material things that we cannot afford. Perhaps I'll start wearing it in another thirty years when we hit the big sixty! Dave Ramsey says, "When you spend your money on paper and on purpose each month with a written budget, you'll actually experience more freedom than before!" If you don't have such a financial plan, make it your anniversary gift to each other, along with a beautiful ream of paper.

I have already referred to the issue of finances on more than one occasion. You are aware of the importance of wisdom in regard to your income and expenses. I write about personal finances in a number of chapters, not only because financial problems can be a core part of marital strife but also because character, personal integrity, and perhaps, to an even greater extent, faith and trust are tied so strongly to the ways we use our finances.

When we feel a strong compulsion to fund the illusion of success, what are we hoping to gain? What does this compulsion say about where we have placed our faith and trust? The illusion can be looked at as an insatiable monster—the more you feed it, the more it begs to be fed. Getting caught up in this cycle doesn't improve your lifestyle; instead, this cycle diminishes your quality of life and impacts your character, integrity, and peace of mind. Set your marriage on a solid financial footing early on by taking charge of your finances as a couple. Down the road you will be very glad you did!

Couple Activity

- How will you work together to overcome the persuasive power of the illusion of success?
- Make it a high priority over the next few days to create a mutually agreed-upon budget.

Day 14

Building Goodwill

The wisdom of the prudent is to give thought to their ways.
—Proverbs 14:8

Proverbs chapter 14 emphasizes the importance of building goodwill and being a truthful witness and not being hotheaded and quick-tempered. I had just read Proverbs 14 when I received a phone call that two of my sons had been involved in a four-car collision just three miles from home. Talk about immediate application!

In such times as these, the wise thing to do is to give thought to our ways. I shot up a prayer, got dressed, and before walking out the door, posted a Facebook message asking others to pray. By the time I got to the scene of the accident, more than forty friends had been praying. This was not the first time I had used social media to ask for prayers; it won't be the last. By the way, the boys were fine (though a bit shaken up). The truck was totaled.

When I returned home, I read verse 30 of Proverbs 14: "A heart at peace gives life to the body." Whether you're at the scene of a car accident with strangers or at home having a disagreement with your wife, the importance of building goodwill cannot be overstated. By our actions, words, and attitudes, we reveal the condition of our hearts. Cars can be replaced, but relationships are not so easily mended. All too often, I find myself counseling soldiers and their spouses struggling with bitterness in relationships that appear lifeless. Without fail, the poison in the relationship originates from one or both spouses failing to give thought to their behavior. This causes them to break down goodwill within the relationship over time.

Some words that *Webster's Dictionary* uses to define goodwill include, "a kindly feeling of approval and support, benevolent concern, cheerful consent, and willing effort." Accountants include goodwill as an intangible asset that increases the book value of a company. Goodwill, or the lack of it, can actually determine the degree of success that a company achieves.

Goodwill in a marriage makes both you and your wife emotionally stronger and leads to positive effects in every other area of your lives. At work, you can focus on the job at hand because you are not preoccupied with problems at home. A marriage steeped in goodwill provides an example for your friends and eventually your children and draws others (including your friends and children) to enjoy spending time with you. Your home becomes a secure fortress and a place for the children to find refuge, as stated in Proverbs 14:26. The ripple effects of a marriage filled with goodwill are almost boundless.

Running a brokerage firm for many years, I fully understood the value of goodwill. In working to create this asset for my company, I saw my new business flourish and enjoyed a high rate of returning customers. I wasn't so quick to recognize goodwill's value and power in my marriage. Goodwill does not wait until the dishwasher is almost empty before it says, "Here, let me help." In our home, such minimal attempts were usually met with an, "I got it now" from Sherry. Mediocre effort doesn't count for much and does very little to build goodwill.

If you ever thought that your wife would make a great Marine drill sergeant, you should consider whether your behavior triggers her need to exert extreme control. For example, if you are always cheerful but have little involvement in ensuring that the household runs smoothly, you are going to foster very little goodwill with your wife. Webster was right: "benevolent concern, cheerful consent, and a willing effort" are absolutely essential to building goodwill.

Goodwill is relatively scarce in society today. As I write these words, I can hear the political campaign ads playing on the TV in my den. Those ads don't contain an ounce of goodwill—not even the "better" candidates' ads are exceptions. Many are filled with negative backbiting foolishness, great exaggerations, and, in many cases, untruths. Is there even one political figure who knows and believes Proverbs 14:9: "goodwill is found among the upright"? Goodwill today is so uncommon that people are suspicious when they do see it. Every day, people are swindled, maybe by a person proclaiming that they have inherited millions from a friend in some foreign country or have been awarded a new roof due to hail damage. Of course in such cases, the windfall is promised after the "lucky" person sends in a ridiculously large processing fee. I see similarities to the campaign ads in these situations and don't wonder that folks tend to be suspicious.

Marriages are susceptible to falling into this mode, too. "Uh oh, he just brought me flowers. It's not my birthday or our anniversary.

What's he up to? What has he done?" Genuine goodwill flows out of a heart that is at peace and thus brings life to others. If your wife is suspicious of your random acts of kindness, take some still, quiet moments with God to explore whether your home lacks peace. In fact, in her own quiet time, your wife may have reflected upon Psalm 55:21: "His talk is smooth as butter, yet war is in his heart; his words are more soothing than oil, yet they are drawn swords," or some other relevant Scripture. Alternately, she may have noted that you have made many feeble attempts in the past to build peace in the home but have failed so; she simply finds it hard to believe that anything will ever change. The words of Jeremiah 6:14 ring loud and clear: "They dress the wound of my people as though it were not serious. 'Peace, peace,' they say, when there is no peace."

Peace produces goodwill, and goodwill produces peace. For the man seeking to improve his marriage, the desire to foster goodwill can be quite frustrating. A vicious cycle can be at play: You want to win her approval by acts of goodwill, but you're frustrated by her suspicion. You don't get the response you had hoped for, so you end up having less peace than before, and you stop trying. Such a cycle can sap your energy. I know. I have experienced this situation myself and have had plenty of deep, soul-searching conversations with other men struggling with the same dilemma.

I recall one such conversation with a man at a weekend men's retreat. I'll call him Marty, because I felt like I was in a *Back to the Future* remake, talking to myself just a few years earlier. First, let me explain how men's retreats typically work. A bunch of guys get together to camp alongside a river or stay at a nice mountain lodge. Some of them are glad to be there; others are not so sure. They generally include fellowship, talking about what it means to be a man, listening to motivational speakers, praying, and maybe some personal reflection with God. The ones that are new get all excited and pumped up. God speaks in many ways; the participants are spiritually refreshed.

The problem comes when the new guy goes home all excited and tells his wife about everything he learned, the changes that have overcome him, and his confidence that their lives will be better from now on as a result of what he's learned. Unfortunately "from now on" always seems to last a week, perhaps two, and then he is back to his old ways of doing things. In the words of Yogi Berra, "It's déjà vu all over again."

I remember walking down the aisle at a Christian college students' retreat in Ridgecrest, North Carolina in the summer of 1983. I had done the same thing in the summer of 1982, but this time I vowed that things would be different. This time I meant it. In a deep pastoral tone, the preacher asked, "Son, why are you here tonight?" With tears streaming down my face, I blurted, "I'm here because I need to recommit to my recommitment."

In talking with Marty, I discovered that his story was virtually identical to mine. He had been to a weekend retreat the year before and made promises to his wife that fell through within days. This time, however, things were much worse. She was tired of the broken promises. This guy was dangerously close to No Man's Land. I gave him this advice: "When you get home in the morning, greet her as you normally do when you have been away and ask her how her weekend was. Then, listen like you have never listened before. Afterward, go about your business."

"But what if she asks me about my weekend?" Marty wanted to know.

"Tell her what you did. Say, 'We had some speakers, watched some movie clips, ate some hamburgers, and smoked cigars around the fire; that's about it.' She'll probably say, 'Well, that's nice.' Then go about your business."

"But—" said Marty.

"No buts, Marty. The bottom line is you've made promise after promise and haven't kept a one. She's had enough of your broken promises. Just go about your business," I said.

Marty responded, "That's it? Have you got a Bible verse to back that up? That's what I need to know, because I have been trying to do everything the Bible says to do."

"Well Marty, since you asked, I think I do. Jesus told a story in Matthew 21," I answered.

There was a man who had two sons. He went to the first and said, "Son, go and work today in the vineyard."

"I will not," he answered but later he changed his mind and went. Then the father went to the other son and said the same thing. He answered, "I will, sir," but he did not go. Which of the two did what his father wanted?

"The first," Marty answered.

"Marty, you have been that second son. You have been telling your wife what you were going to do, but you haven't done it. Can you see why she would be upset with you?" I asked.

Many men are just like Marty—good guys that want to do what's right. I know I was and still am in some ways. You may even be able to quote the Bible like Marty, chapter and verse. However, to be the kind of husband the Bible calls us to be, more is required to build goodwill within our marriages. Thinking about your behavior is a way to recognize that you need God's power, that you are totally, 100 percent, dependent on His strength working in you. Otherwise, you are like the apostle Paul when he said, "I do not understand what I do. For what I want to do, I do not do, but what I hate, I do" (Romans 7:15).

Weekend men's retreats are great; they can even be a turning point in many men's lives, but if we leave thinking that we are going to make all these life-transforming changes, then we have missed the point altogether. Getting fired up is not a bad thing. Doing so can be fun and get the endorphins flowing so that we actually feel better physically and mentally for a while. When the newness wears off, however, we can easily fall back into old, lazy patterns.

Your wife is not interested in any more broken promises; in fact, you have probably experienced her wrath when you say the words, "I promise." You certainly aren't building any goodwill by making promises that you don't keep. Such unfulfilled promises lead to the exact opposite of goodwill. Stop making promises to her about how you are going to change. Instead, get alone with God, and build goodwill with Him. This work with God is the starting point for building goodwill with your wife. Ask Him to change you. Your attempts to change yourself are not working. We'll develop this thought more in the days ahead. For now, be encouraged that you are on your way. You are here right now, but you'll be "there" soon.

Couple Activity

- Ask her how you can best demonstrate goodwill in your marriage. Don't make any promises; just work on building goodwill.
- Do you have a tendency to be quick-tempered, lazy, or indifferent? If so, how might these traits create problems?
- When the challenges come, how will "giving thought to your ways" guide you?

Day 15

Think Before You Speak

A gentle answer turns away wrath,
but a harsh word stirs up anger.
—Proverbs 15:1

Think before you speak! Learn this one early on, and save yourself a world of woe. I am fortunate to be married to a great cook, but the first month of marriage I made the mistake of comparing Sherry's green beans to my mom's, which are cooked with a ham bone and other seasonings. I immediately recognized the error of my ways. According to Proverbs 15:2 and 4, "The tongue of the wise adorns knowledge, but the mouth of the fool gushes folly; the soothing tongue is a tree of life, but a perverse tongue crushes the spirit." Sherry didn't respond with words; she didn't have to. Proverbs 15:3 tells us, "A happy heart makes the face cheerful, but heartache crushes the spirit." A woman's countenance is an incredibly accurate indicator of the health of the relationship, not just at the dinner table but in daily life. If we aim to build goodwill by giving thought to our ways, we do well to consider the words we use along the way.

Words have tremendous power! With our words, we stir up conflict or calm quarrels; we hurt or we heal; and we build up, or we tear down. By the spoken word, God created the universe; statesmen established nations; and generals rallied troops. In marriage, you create an environment of love and strength by your kind, thoughtful words. Not surprisingly, Philippians 4:8–9 says, "Finally, brothers and sisters, whatever is true, whatever is noble, whatever is right, whatever is pure, whatever is lovely, whatever is admirable—if anything is excellent or praiseworthy—think about such things." What we dwell on is what we will ultimately speak, so think before you begin talking.

Often in my counseling and in my own marriage, I apply an acrostic I learned from Andy Stanley: "THINK: Is it *truthful*? Is it *helpful*? Is it *inspiring*? Is it *necessary*? Is it *kind*?" If I can't answer yes to all five questions, I probably need to do some more thinking and simply keep my mouth shut.

Some may say, "Well, does that mean I should be oblivious to the facts when challenges do come?" The short answer is no. I'm not suggesting denying facts but rather recognizing a choice between a gentle answer or a harsh word. So many times, I hear couples in counseling who want to get the facts straight. Sometimes you have to stop looking at the facts. Be done with this he said/she said stuff. Proverbs 15:23 tells us, "There is joy in giving a fitting reply." No marriage is perfect, but through grace some appear to be so. By God's design, marriage is that place where grace, love, forgiveness, and redemption should shine the brightest.

When you are faced with a relationship challenge in which your wife is not ready to talk, count it as a blessing that she is thinking before she speaks. She doesn't want to hurt you. Men, on the other hand, have a desire to fix things and a tendency to barrel ahead. Then we are vexed when the problem is not resolved. Think before you speak.

On the other hand, if you feel hurt by your wife's words, you can respond to this hurt in a godly way. I know I have been hard on you men in some ways, but it's better that I am your drill instructor instead of your wife. Inevitably she will say or do hurtful things, sometimes seemingly without cause. These words and actions may often appear to you as a preemptive first strike. I contend that the majority of the time, her hurtful behaviors originate from her own hurts—perhaps even some that you generate.

Sometimes the harshness of words comes not so much from the words themselves but rather from the ways in which we speak them. When you talk in a booming voice or with sarcasm, or talk down to your spouse, you shouldn't be surprised at the chilling effect this behavior has on all aspects of the relationship. Passion quickly fades when the relationship lacks compassion. Compassion is considered in many of the world religions to be one of the highest virtues. In Christianity, it is the cornerstone of the golden rule of Luke 6:31, "Do to others as you would have them do to you." When you demonstrate compassion toward your spouse with the words you say and how you say them, you strengthen your identity with your spouse. Her passion for you will be heightened by your compassion for her.

Couple Activity

- Share with each other some examples of times when the other has spoken compassionately and given encouragement in a difficult situation. Remember to repeat such words of encouragement and love whenever you get the opportunity. Express gratitude when your spouse does the same.

- Discuss and agree to some basic "rules of engagement" that will guide you through challenging times.

Day 16

Whatever You Do

Commit to the Lord whatever you do,
and He will establish your plans.
—Proverbs 16:3

Most likely the day you said "I do," you committed to honor and
cherish your wife "till death do we part." After thirty-five years
of marriage, an interviewer asked Ruth Graham if she had ever
considered divorcing her husband, evangelist Billy Graham. She
responded, "No, I've never thought of divorce, but, I did think of
murder a few times."

In September 2013, a woman pushed her husband over a cliff eight
days after their wedding. Recently a doctor in Indiana killed his wife
and himself the day of their wedding in a heated argument concerning
the prenuptial agreement. While Ruth Graham was joking, these
other individuals obviously had some very serious issues in their
relationships.

Proverbs 16 offers valuable truths for the marriage relationship and
any relationship for that matter. A day comes to every marriage when

questions arise; feelings are hurt; and tempers flare. In such times, we struggle to remember the feelings of love and commitment we felt so strongly the day we said "I do."

While the relationship principles that we cover in this book can help any couple, some can only be grasped by those who are committed to the Lord. Almost any reasonable person can grasp that his own motives are not always pure. Sometimes we do what we do, just because we want to. Sometimes we say things that sting, because in our own hurt we want to hurt others. Faith is required in order to believe Proverbs 16:4, "The Lord works out everything to its proper end." Verse 6 states, "Through love and faithfulness sin is atoned for … evil is avoided." Lastly, you must call on faith to know that "When the Lord takes pleasure in anyone's way, he causes their enemies to make peace with them" (Proverbs 16:7). This peacemaking applies to friction with your wife as well.

We can avoid much evil and heartache in relationships by knowing how forgiveness works. Don't jump to the conclusion that I am simply saying you must be a forgiving person. Self-righteousness is always quick to say "I forgive" then seeks to prove that it does so by going to a person who has offended, piously yelling, "I forgive you!"

Three problems come with that approach. First, the individual may not even realize he or she has offended you. Second, if this person is aware but you declare your forgiveness before he or she has realized a need or desire for it, you will likely incite him or her to further anger. Third, and perhaps most importantly, forgiveness that arises out of self-righteousness fails to see its own need to be forgiven and is really no forgiveness at all but rather a form of control and hypocrisy.

After graduation I worked on staff at the seminary, where Sherry and I became good friends with a new professor and his wife. We would double-date. The professor and I worked out together; he was even the first nonfamily member to hold our firstborn son on the day of his birth. His wife invited Sherry to partner with her in a multilevel business opportunity. Sherry had no interest in doing so. From that day forward, he no longer worked out with me, and they wouldn't go to dinner with us. In the halls of the school, he would avoid me at every turn. In my heart, I wanted to tell him off for treating us that way. In my self-righteousness, I wanted to tell him "I forgive you!" just to show him I was a bigger man than he.

Then I read Proverbs 16:24, "Gracious words are a honeycomb, sweet to the soul and healing to the bones." I went by his office to visit him. He just sat there. I spoke his name and then said, "I have come to ask for *your* forgiveness. I have been angry and upset that our relationship is not what it used to be and am very sorry for my feelings." He didn't say anything but looked down at his desk.

When I turned to go, he said, "No, Ken, you are not the one who needs forgiveness. I am." He got up, came around his desk, and hugged me. I walked out of that office with tears streaming down my cheek. The relationship was restored. I can't pat myself on the back because I did the right thing. I didn't do what I did because I'm a good person. Apart from the grace of God, I would never have gone to the man in the manner I did.

Wisdom has taught me that, apart from His grace, I will never be the husband, father, son, or friend that God calls me to be. God calls us to do the things we can't do. Wisdom teaches us to run to Him so that we can do what we would not and could not do without Him. Until

71

you stop believing that you're nearly perfect and everyone else has issues or should be asking for forgiveness, you will always be one step away from where God wants you to be. You must address the issues of your heart, or you will never understand the importance of reconciliation, the need for repentance, the power of forgiveness, or the joy of living the resurrection life.

What is a relationship but words and actions? And what incredible power do they have? With our words and actions we can build up or we can destroy. When we are hurt and offended, we can demonstrate grace in our response so that we open the door to healing and transformation. We can convey forgiveness in a manner that is gracious and humble. Such is the case not only between husbands and wives but also between parents and children. We'll give more consideration to the parent-child relationship on day 28. For now, consider the following couple activity and verses on forgiveness.

Couple Activity

- In the past when you have been hurt or offended by your spouse, what has been your typical response?
- How will you seek to respond in the future when such times arise?
- Do you have one or more places of pain right now where the healing process can begin to take place though the act of genuinely forgiving your spouse?

For if you forgive other people when they sin against you, your heavenly Father will also forgive you. But if you do not forgive others their sins, your Father will not forgive your sins.
—Matthew 6:14–15

If we confess our sins, He is faithful and just and will forgive us our sins and purify us from all unrighteousness.
—1 John 1:9

Repent, then, and turn to God, so that your sins may be wiped out, that times of refreshing may come from the Lord.
—Acts 3:19

Day 17

The Test

The crucible for silver and the furnace for gold,
but the Lord tests the heart.
—Proverbs 17:3

I really didn't know what I was made of until I was forty-five years old. Till then, I had lived a happy, carefree life for the most part. Sure, we had the challenges that are common to every marriage—raising kids, paying the bills, and occasionally arguing, but I always believed that I had a strong level of personal resilience and knew that I had my faith. Sherry had even more of these qualities than I did. During this time my mettle was tested through a series of events that rocked my world and brought me to my knees.

As the waves of despair crashed over me, I found myself spiraling down a dark hole that I had never known. Thoughts of suicide bombarded me virtually every moment. My oldest son was the first to intervene. He could see that his dad was not the dad he had always known. Just a few years earlier, I had been setting bench-press records and running a successful real estate company. When the economy imploded, so did my house of cards. I felt like a failure whose family would be better off without me. Had it not been for the prayers of my wife and the love of my sons—well, I shudder to think.

We all have tests to take. You don't graduate from school without passing at least a few of them. When those tests come in life, realize that they are not a result of God hating you or being angry at you, or necessarily a result of sin. They are part of everyone's life.

Jesus plainly tells us, "In this world you will have trouble." (John 16:33). I have no need to give a theological defense of why a good and loving God would allow bad things to happen. I leave that task to others. However, I will say that those things I once thought of as tragic events I now consider truly divine appointments. In my case, I experienced God as provider, sustainer, and restorer of peace.

You may find yourself in the middle of tests right now. Maybe your health, finances, or, perhaps, your relationship with your spouse is suffering. The situation may be very ugly and involve infidelity. Or you could be aware that you have simply grown apart. I don't know your situation, but I do know that God is in the resurrection business. He is able to take that which is lifeless and give it life. He can restore hope. He can renew the joy you once had. Your situation may be such that you are looking at all the bad in your marriage and are ready to say, "I'm done." Deeply in your heart, however, you hold on to a hope that maybe, just maybe, things can get better. I say to you, that ember of hope is the finger of God. In Matthew 17:20, Jesus tells us that if we have faith the size of a mustard seed, we can move mountains. If God can bring life from nothing, certainly He can restore the life in relationships.

In John 5, we learn that on the streets of Jerusalem, Jesus encountered a man who had been an invalid for thirty-eight years. Jesus asked him a question, "Do you want to get well?"

At first the man was full of excuses: "I can't do it; no one will help me; others are in the way ..." Jesus responded, "Get up! Pick up your mat and walk." We can talk all day long about wanting a better marriage, but the walk has got to match the talk. God expects you to do certain things, and so does your wife. If you want to pass the test, you had best start studying up on what those things are.

As I write, our master bathroom is a total wreck. I pulled wallpaper off a week ago, leaving an unsightly mess. Sherry says it looks like a crack house. She is now worried that it will be next spring before the project is done. I am committing to her and to you that the bathroom will look new, with a fresh coat of paint, before Thanksgiving, which is just a few weeks from now. How's that for jumping out on a limb?

The "honey do" list is not the only thing you need to focus on. What have we been studying the past seventeen days? I make the same challenge to you that I have made to my sons from the time they could talk. What's the most important thing? Be a man, a man of God who knows the importance of wisdom and pursues it as the most valued treasure to possess. Start looking for the good. Begin applying yourself to understand your wife, or, at the very least, to connect with her heart. Think before you speak. When you do speak, make sure your words and tone allow her to receive you message joyfully. Don't ever try to make her the brunt of your stupid jokes. If she were to laugh, she would only do so to save you embarrassment. If you haven't already cleaned out the dishwasher when you first get into the kitchen, jump to it the moment you hear a glass clinking.

Oh, and another thing … you may be a very spiritual person, but don't use your faith as an excuse. "I've got to write my book, read my Bible, pray …" What she really needs you to do is to take out the trash or clean up the dog pile she just ran over in the garage. If you have stepped in the proverbial pile through infidelity, you may be experiencing your greatest test. To you, I would say that God is the God of forgiveness. Furthermore, you are no worse in deed than I, nor any other man has been in thought. Jesus said in Matthew 5:28, "I tell you that anyone who looks at a woman lustfully has already committed adultery with her in his heart." The great test for you is in believing that God is the God of resurrection power, that He can restore that which is broken.

If you are a woman reading these words and have suffered through your husband's infidelity, I can only imagine the sense of betrayal that has broken your heart. You should never have to take such a test; however, I do know many women, and some men, who have had to do so. Some chose divorce while others had divorce forced upon them, against their will and desire for reconciliation. In any case, such a situation always presents a test, similar to the one Jesus experienced in the garden the night he was betrayed. Would he take the steps necessary to open the door of forgiveness for the world? Perhaps our greatest test as humans is whether we are willing to forgive when we are wronged.

Couple Activity

- Where is the finger of God touching your heart just now?
- How has God revealed His character to you in a time of testing?

Day 18

Sometimes You Just Need to Listen

To answer before listening—that is folly and shame.
—Proverbs 18:13

As we consider this next subject, I am reminded of the scene in *Rocky III* ...

Interviewer: What's your prediction for the fight?
Clubber Lang: My prediction?
Interviewer: Yes, your prediction.
[*Clubber looks into camera.*]
Clubber Lang: Pain!

We have learned that "a gentle answer turns away wrath." Before you even think about answering your wife, realize that sometimes all you need to do is listen. Also, contrary to popular opinion, the reason you should do so is not that women have a need to talk more than men. *Science Magazine* reported several university studies in 2007, revealing that men and women, on average, actually speak about the same number of words each day. I am guessing the myth that women talk more than men has been perpetuated to explain why men have difficulty communicating with their partners. Sorry men, but I have to call it how I see it. We men experience much unnecessary pain simply from the words we speak. Proverbs 18:6 says, "The lips of fools bring them strife, and their mouths invite a beating." I would take three rounds in the ring with Clubber Lang if doing so would erase all the pain I have caused by my foolish words.

The same 2007 studies revealed that women tend to talk about others, whereas men talk about things (cars, hunting, sports stats, etc.). Even so, we need to be careful not to stereotype her talk as gossip. Wake up, guys. The goal here is to build a loving relationship with your wife, which is kind of difficult to do when you accuse her of being a gossip. Choose to take the high road. She is talking about the things that are important to her, many of which revolve around people. Honestly, when was the last time your relationship was strengthened and really went to a deeper level simply because your team won the Super Bowl?

I have learned far more from listening than I ever have from talking. Unfortunately listening is one of the most challenging skills for men, including me. A while back, I began to realize how often I would take over my wife's stories in social settings. I realize now that I was crushing her and am reminded of Proverbs 18:14, "The human spirit can endure in sickness, but a crushed spirit who can bear?"

When I saw this fault in my own life, I also became much more aware of it in other men. We may accuse women of loving to talk, but the communication problems we have with our wives may be more a result of our loving to hear ourselves talk and to be in control. For example, in private conversation with her, I began to realize how often I would speak over her or give her answers when she wasn't looking for them. Worst of all, I realized that even when I wasn't pontificating, I wasn't really listening. Have you ever noticed that flaw in others? You can see that they are thinking as you are talking; however, they are not thinking about what you are saying but rather about what they are going to say next. Again, wake up, guys— multitasking is not our domain. Even if you think you can, don't do so—not with your wife, anyway, not when she needs to talk. Think about it. How long would you last on the job if you kept staring at the computer screen or the sports page when the boss was trying to engage you in conversation? Can we say, "Folly and shame and likely a pink slip?"

For two years of our marriage while I was serving as the interim pastor in a little country church in a town of three hundred, Sherry and I would spend every Sunday with my aunt and uncle. After lunch we would put the two boys down for a nap and talk with Uncle Freeman and Aunt Eva Mae. In all that time I literally never heard them say a negative word about anyone. That was over twenty years ago. Recently I recalled those days to my cousin, John. He confirmed that his parents were as I have described them. John said, "They always gave folks the benefit of the doubt." I find myself wanting to be like them as I get older. When I find myself reverting to my old ways, I cry "Uncle" and mean it literally!

Active listening to your wife includes paying attention and reflecting back what she has said, so that she knows you have heard her. Refrain from offering a quick-fix response when she wants to express her feelings about a difficult situation. If she says something about what you are doing or not doing, avoid rolling your eyes or responding with sarcastic words. Probably most importantly, watch the tone of your voice. Learning the art of listening will reap incredible benefits for your marriage. In fact, listening is the starting point for giving thought to your actions, building goodwill, and answering appropriately when it is time to speak.

Sometimes listening also means silence. Sherry is very comfortable riding down the road with me without feeling the need to speak. I used to think her silence was due to anger; thus I would worry that I had done something wrong. I have learned better that it is part of her quiet, gentle way. I have come to greatly appreciate just being in her presence. Her demeanor reminds me of Psalm 46:10, one of my favorite parts of Scripture: "Be still, and know that I am God."

If you have ever been described as "a talker," think twice before taking it as a compliment. Don't be quick to rebut with, "Well, I am just a friendly person and enjoy talking to people." Actually, the person who says you are a talker may feel like you are talking at them rather than with them. If others have said you're a talker, it may be that God is trying to put his finger on an area of your character that He wants to refine. A refined person is described as one who chooses words carefully, doesn't ramble, and knows how to listen.

A number of years ago Mother Teresa was asked what she said to God when she prayed. She replied: "I don't say anything. I just listen." When the interviewer asked what she heard God saying, Mother Teresa answered, "He doesn't say anything. He just listens. And if you can't understand that, I can't explain it to you."

One final thought for today: Don't preach at your spouse. When you feel the urge to quote Scripture at your wife, quote it to yourself instead. Live out what you are quoting. Then, you won't have to quote it to her, because she will want to learn it and live it, too. The same goes for women. The first book of Peter addresses such situations. In it, spiritual women are married to ungodly men, and the Scripture demonstrates that these men may be won over to God without words but through the behavior of their wives, when they see their purity and reverence. I can't help but think this relationship principle applies equally to men. Sometimes you just need to listen.

Couple Activity

- Ask her to tell you what good communication looks like to her. What does it look like to you?
- What changes do you need to make now that will strengthen your skills at listening?

Day 19

Loving Life with Your Wife

One who gets wisdom loves life;
the one who cherishes understanding will soon prosper.
—Proverbs 19:8

Sometimes we men just don't get it. *Success Magazine* ran an article in 2008 on the top twenty-five books about success. The top three are recognized as classics in corporate America and have been read by millions of people, yet the authors of each experienced divorce, one of them twice. One had an affair, while another left his wife and baby in his search for success. When the latter man reunited with his wife seventeen years later, the marriage lasted a short while before ending again in divorce. All three men are now dead, leaving behind all their accolades and worldly wealth.

These men did cherish understanding of certain things. They had a keen understanding of finances, corporate negotiations, and money-making strategies, and they prospered in those areas. Perhaps they even loved the life they created for themselves. Yet we all know men who would confess at the pinnacle of their corporate success that they had lost the things that really mattered the most. The divorce courts and movies are filled with such stories.

How many times have we heard the words or said them ourselves, "I'll never understand my wife." This explanation, becomes our mantra (excuse) for not even trying to understand. How many times have we heard the words, "You don't even try to understand"? Interestingly wisdom in Proverbs is personified as feminine, while Solomon writes in Ecclesiastes that trying to understand wisdom is like "chasing the wind." These insights might help us to understand why we may at times feel as if we are chasing the wind when we are trying to understand our wives! We miss the main point with this focus, though. Regardless of how much we as men are able to understand, we can always gain greater understanding. We can never fully grasp all the benefits to be gained in seeking wisdom or a greater understanding and appreciation of the one we promised to love and cherish. Cherishing your wife is cherishing wisdom; cherishing wisdom is cherishing your wife. The two go hand-in-hand.

Only in very recent years have I come to more fully appreciate the beautiful complexity of the female mind, especially my wife's. In so doing, I have found that this greater appreciation of her thoughts, rather than my understanding of them, means that I am loving life with my wife more than ever before. I have benefited greatly from her instincts, insights, and multidimensional way of viewing the world. The benefits have spilled over into relationships with my children, mom, family, and friends. Such a phenomenon shows how "one who gets wisdom loves life." With wisdom, we not only keep ourselves from stumbling over stupidity; we mellow. We don't get stressed over things we can do nothing about.

At fifty-one years of age, I am starting to love the journey again. I am also realizing the wisdom of something that an older man shared with me when I was young, "You'll be here where I am a lot faster than you think." Time is flying by—life is like a vapor. I am still not where I want to be, but I am getting there. You are getting to your desired destination, too.

When my sister and I were kids, my dad would play a cruel joke on us as we traveled to Florida for vacation. We would usually start off at five in the morning. Leanne and I would crawl in the back of the station wagon to sleep and every so often pop our heads up to ask, "Are we there yet? Are we there?"

Dad would say, "No, we're not there yet." An hour later he would yell out with great excitement, "We're here!" We would pop up again, ready to hit the beach only to discover that we were at the state line with four more hours to go.

"Daddy we're not there," we would say.

"That's right; we're here," would be his answer.

"But you said we were there."

"No, I didn't; I said we were here, When we get there we'll be here."

"Oh, Daddy."

"Go back to sleep, kids."

Here you are. Maybe you have had some bumps along the way. Learn to practice the art of enjoying the journey, and wake up to the reality that God has given you an incredible traveling partner. You'll be there soon enough—much faster than you think.

Couple Activity

- Ask her how you can demonstrate that you cherish her way of thinking.
- Ask her to point out one way that you can improve how you relate to others. Step out of your comfort zone, and be aware of how you can put into practice what she reveals.
- What will your life together look like when you get there—ten, twenty, or thirty years from now?

Day 20

Avoiding Strife

It is to one's honor to avoid strife,
but every fool is quick to quarrel.
—Proverbs 20:3

In our third year of marriage Sherry and I made the four-hundred-mile ride back to Atlanta to visit family for Christmas. A time that should have been a joyful occasion proved to be anything but, all because of my stubborn desire to do things my way. Sherry wanted to stay with her family; I wanted to stay with mine. I asserted and abused my personal power to the highest degree by making the decision for "us" that we would stay with neither family. Since we couldn't decide where to stay, we would get a motel room. Any man with sense should see, just as I see now, that this decision did not work to support fellowship in our marriage. Instead, the decision was all about me and what I wanted.

Sadly the occasion wasn't the first, nor the last, where I acted foolishly and selfishly in our marriage. Like most men, I have had much to learn on an emotional level in order to help build a mature, joyful marriage. God can change a man. That's the power of the gospel.

He can take a man with a heart of stone and fill that heart with His grace and love.

When a law enforcement officer tells a bad guy to "freeze," he is exercising legitimate power. When a prosecutor successfully prosecutes the bad guy, he is demonstrating expert power. When a parent extends Friday-night curfew to a son who brought home a good report card, he is using reward power. All of these are acceptable uses of power, given the circumstances. On the other hand, applying such power to your relationship with your wife will quickly backfire. She is not a criminal, just because she disagrees with you. If you treat her like one, she will avoid you like one. You may be a skilled orator who can successfully prosecute a case in the courtroom, but marriage won't flourish in an environment of legalism. Use of reward power may work on your kids, but it's no way to treat your wife. She's not your child. Treating her as if she is will lead to her growing out of wanting or needing what you have to offer, just as your kids do in the natural course of life.

Men, even as little boys, have this innate desire to jockey for position; we use various means of power to do so. We engage in competition on the playground and on the sports field, as well as in the courtroom, the boardroom, the neighborhood, and even in the church. When we apply the same techniques and attitude to our marriage, however, we lose. Let that observation sink in. When your goal is to win the argument with your spouse, *you lose*!

Proverbs 20:6 says, "Many claim to have unfailing love, but a faithful person who can find?" We men have a hard time saying the word *love*, unless of course we're talking about fishing, hunting, golf, football, or some other activity. Expressing our love to and for a person, especially unfailing love—well, that makes us feel vulnerable. We fear rejection and do not want to be viewed as weak.

We do a great job, or so we think, of expressing our emotion of anger, because anger is a "manly" response to being wronged. If I can beat my chest on the playground and beat you in everything else, I'm the dominant male, the leader of the pack. We carry that attitude into our marriage, thinking it will work, but it doesn't. The softer feelings of compassion and empathy are in us; we've just stuffed them way down to protect our manly ego. We have to make a conscious effort to draw on those emotions to help strengthen our marriages and, in turn, make us strong men in all spheres of our lives (as we've discussed on previous days).

In my work with veterans, we have developed a program called the Courageous Project to address the issue of moral injuries that many have experienced as a result of war. Our goal is to provide a place where these men can be transparent with their feelings and experiences. We go a step beyond dealing with the issues of post-traumatic stress disorder (PTSD) to gently handling the issues of the heart. Just this weekend, I worked with fourteen veterans in a workshop sponsored by AMVET bikers to help them learn the skills that can save lives. Everyone present had been impacted in some way by the moral injury of war or the loss of a battle buddy due to suicide or an enemy hand. As we went around the room, each of them began to share their stories, many of them with tears. Call it their "feminine side" if you must. I call it being real. These were courageous men who have faithfully served their country. They continue to demonstrate that courage and compassion here at home in working to save their brothers. I am reminded of the words in John 15:13: "Greater love has no one than this: to lay down one's life for one's friends." Jesus did so with great passion motivated by love. He gave his life to save the world from sin, but the agents of his death were highly critical of who he claimed to be.

You may think your wife is your biggest critic. So what? You probably deserve her criticism to some degree. Even if you believe the criticism is unmerited, seek to learn from it. Look for the good; consider your response; and be a better man because of her feedback. Don't forfeit the game by allowing your ego to get in the way.

One Sunday afternoon after I had received many accolades from church members from that morning's sermon, I noticed that Sherry had not said a word. When I inquired, she responded, "They don't know you like I do." Talk about a wakeup call. Sherry's not a critical wife, so her response was especially tough to hear, but she was spot-on. Lesson learned.

Avoiding strife does not mean living in denial, which can result in failure to forgive and to heal from emotional wounds. I am also not asking you to deny your identity as a man. On the contrary, I'm asking you to fulfill that identity. Many men experience moral injury on the field of battle because they participated in or witnessed something that violated their personal moral code. In a sense, their brokenness is a loss of identity. War is a terrible thing. One can fight with honor, in a way that minimizes the potential for moral injury and loss of identity. The same holds true in marriage.

Disagreeing with your wife and intentionally creating strife are different things. When we hold spite in our hearts and use hateful words, we create moral injury within the marriage. At the very least, we burn relationship bridges that are meant to keep us connected. In difficult situations, we can react in ways to honor the other, rather than to dishonor. Learn the difference. Doing so will be a blessing to your relationship and to your own sense of identity and honor.

Couple Activity

- In what ways have you recognized your defensiveness when you and your partner disagree?
- Describe a time when you were more focused on the "me" rather than the "us" in your relationship.
- Brainstorm with your partner ways that you can show respect to each other during times of disagreement.

Note: Our goal is not to focus on past hurts, but hopefully after twenty days of working through the couple's activities, you understand the purpose of such exercises. We're looking for a little bit of self-reflection that can help spur personal growth and strengthen the relationship. It's not about one spouse reminding the other spouse of how defensive the other is, but it is about you recognizing within yourself those things that hinder the relationship so that you will be able to better navigate around such potholes in the future.

Day 21

My Way or the Highway

A person may think their own ways are right,
but the Lord weighs the heart.
—Proverbs 21:2

Alexander Pope, in *Essays on Criticism,* first penned the words in 1709 that have now been used in various works over the past three hundred years: "Fools rush in where angels fear to tread." I am reminded of this quote as I consider my own words and the words of Proverbs 21.

Over the past twenty-one days, my focus has been directed toward men. I have challenged you to step up and fulfill our calling as men and husbands. I think of three men right now who need encouragement in their marriages. To each, I recommended a book that squarely places the responsibility on the man for the condition of his marriage. I concur with the author and have greatly benefited myself from reading it.

The first man bought the book and is working to apply the principles. He and his wife appear more hopeful; her countenance has improved greatly. The second man bought the book, but because it's not a Christian book written in King James language, he is not interested in finishing it. Their marriage appears still to be at a crossroad that could go either way. Her countenance remains as it has been for some time. The third man has yet to buy the book. In his last correspondence, he confided, "Things are bad and getting worse."

Now I tread "where angels fear to tread." Hopefully I have prefaced my entry fairly with a call to action by men and am not rushing in like a fool. Ladies, I know your greatest challenge in life is your husband. Guys, if you're honest, you will admit that I'm right. Just as I have challenged and even hammered the men, so now I challenge the wives.

Wives can hold a "my way or the highway" attitude, just like many men can. Often in counseling couples, I actually encourage the wife to maintain such an attitude. In those times when the man refuses to get help for a drinking problem, cease his philandering ways, or read a book that would help the marriage, the wife's setting stringent boundaries is critical for the health of the marriage and its two partners. Otherwise, the wife is enabling the codependent dysfunction and setting herself up for further heartache and pain and perhaps even physical harm.

Some situations warrant a woman's saying, "This is how it is going to be." Sorry, guys. I know you thought that was something only you could say, because you are the "man of the house." I've never really understood a man making that assertion in the first place—"I'm the man of the house." Do you mean to distinguish that she's not the man of the house; you are the head of the house; or you are the leader in *your* home? Okay, good for you—then lead. Lead by being the first one to change. What did Rocky say after beating the giant Russian? "If I can change and you can change, we can all change." Don't give any more excuses related to her not trying or not changing. You change. Till then, I side with her "this is how it's going to be" approach.

Ladies, in saying all this to him, I'm not suggesting that you turn up the heat. You don't have permission to beat him over the head with the book he refuses to read. Don't even remind him about the book. The wisdom I challenge him to depend upon is the same wisdom I call you to depend upon. The Lord tests the heart. Are you looking for the good and speaking the truth in love? Are you seeking to win him over with your gentle ways? A "my way or the highway" attitude is needed in some situations, but not all, especially not when it is held with great fury and disdain. James was writing to both men and women in James 1:19 when he said, "My dear brothers and sisters, take note of this: Everyone should be quick to listen, slow to speak and slow to become angry, because human anger does not produce the righteousness that God desires."

Has all your righteous indignation really produced the results you desired? Alternately, is he retreating to the desert (basement, bar, friendly female coworker's office, or other refuge)? Some wives may say, "I want him as far away as possible, and I really could not care less what he does anymore." Do you really want that outcome? Did you want it the day you stood before the minister and said "I do"? Did you "promise to love and to cherish him" or just stay with him for the sake of the kids so they could see what a bad marriage looks like? I suspect your desire is the former. I also suspect that since you have read this far, the finger of God has touched that ember of hope within your own heart. As a woman of faith, you still believe "with God all things are possible." Though Christ was speaking about salvation in these words from Matthew 19:26, He said them immediately following His discourse on divorce. If God can save the worst of sinners, certainly He can save your marriage.

The principles of Proverbs apply equally to women and men. In fact, this book of the Bible concludes with the thoughts of a woman and a further challenge to wives and husbands that a successful marriage takes two.

Couple Activity

- Share with your partner something good that he or she brings to the relationship, whether it be a consistently uplifting way of expressing love, a steadfast attention to keeping the household running smoothly, or some other gift. Think of ways you can continue to express your appreciation to your partner for the positive things he or she does in your daily lives.
- Till this point, I have not asked you to pray together as a couple. Hopefully you have been doing so all along. Today's activity is to pray with each other, asking God to give you wisdom that will bless your marriage and the strength to follow through on some of those earlier activities that perhaps you were hesitant to consider.

Day 22

The Family Name

A good name is more desirable than great riches;
to be esteemed is better than silver or gold.
—Proverbs 22:1

I grew up in a two-bedroom, one-bathroom home and slept in the basement as a teenager. The town we lived in was recently ranked the crime capital of the state, but it did not have such a notorious distinction forty years ago. I never thought that I was missing anything as I was growing up. Most of the folks I knew from that town have long since moved away. Recently I attended the funeral visitation of a childhood friend I had not seen in thirty years. I was sad for the loss of a friend who had not reached fifty years of age, but I was glad to see his brothers, sister, and mom. Our visit brought back many fond memories of childhood, some of them about my dad.

Though Dad died in 1989 and many I knew from the community have moved to various places, I occasionally run into people who knew him. They often tell me, "Your dad was a good man" or "I loved your dad." When I opened my own real estate company, I needed a business loan. The banker asked me if I was Pete Koon's son. When I said yes, she said, "Well, have a seat, and tell me what you need." No, I never missed out on anything, because I inherited that which is far greater than silver and gold. I think of Dad when I read Proverbs 22.

> A good name is more desirable than great riches; to be esteemed is better than silver or gold. Rich and poor have this in common: The LORD is the Maker of them all ... Humility is the fear of the LORD; its wages are riches and honor and life ... Start children off on the way they should go, and even when they are old they will not turn from it ...

I have to confess, when I left home thirty years ago, I lusted after the nicer things in life. Within a few years, I had a bigger house, wore a diamond ring, and drove a Cadillac. Sherry drove a big SUV. Having nice things is not inherently bad, but nowadays I'm not as interested in passing on material things to my kids. Instead, I want to give my kids the inheritance my dad gave me—a good name.

Both husbands and wives have responsibility for the family name. We learn in Proverbs 31 the great value a woman can give to her husband's name and the respect he garners because of her good character. Synergy is created when both husband and wife understand the value of a good name. This positive energy is a blessing to the couple, children of the marriage, and those who know the family. The reputation that the couple creates over time is the foundation for everything covered thus far—honor, integrity, the grace we show, the friendships we make, our problem-solving skills, and our financial acumen.

I had the honor of officiating at the wedding of my firstborn son, MaCrae. Many people commented that it was the most beautiful wedding they had ever attended. The ceremony wasn't extravagant; in fact, it was a very simple wedding, attended by perhaps one hundred friends and family at the chapel at Dobbins Air Force Base. Lauren's sister was the maid of honor, and her friend, Stephanie, a bridesmaid. Nathan (MaCrae's oldest brother) was the best man. Chad and Tyler (his other brothers) served as groomsmen; and cousins Corrie and Amy played the guitar and violin. The guys bought new black suits for the occasion that they can use again, while MaCrae and I wore our military dress uniforms. MaCrae's friends from the Air Force Honor Guard provided the saber arch the Bride and Groom walked through. Lauren did most of the planning with help from her mom; MaCrae scheduled the Dobbins NCO Club; and Sherry and I created and printed the order of service. We decorated the programs with pretty, golden bows. They couple didn't use a wedding coordinator, so at the rehearsal I simply walked them through the steps. Afterward, we said a prayer and went to dinner. The ceremony was simple, yet beautiful! To top it off, just as I introduced them for the first time as husband and wife and they stepped through the saber arch, the Air Force Thunderbirds did a roaring fly-by in formation. At the reception, folks wanted to know how we had arranged Thunderbirds for a wedding. I simply responded, "We have connections in high places." I was only joking, for the timing was a lucky coincidence. For the honeymoon, MaCrae and Lauren scheduled a last-minute two-for-one cruise. The newlyweds stopped by yesterday on their way home to their sweet little two-bedroom, one-bathroom house. I know I'm biased, but I can't help but believe that, even now, this couple is well on their way to understanding the value of a good name.

Wisdom, or the lack of it, is revealed by the things we value. We continually hear stories of men (and some women) "cooking the books" to defraud their employers out of millions. Some have destroyed companies in doing so and hurt many people. These corrupt individuals who lack wisdom deserve the sentences they receive. Most of us would say, "I would never do such a thing." I now recognize many times in my own life, however, when a desire for more caused me to be less than prudent. Wisdom has never failed me, but I have often failed wisdom. Failing to rely on wisdom has led to my buying a juicer I never use, implementing wasteful marketing gimmick that failed in my business, and making other poor choices.

When I first opened my real estate company (prior to the advent of the Internet), I bought an ad in the local phone book. The phone company gave me a call-forwarding number that was exclusive to the phone book. The fees were to be based on the number of calls that came through this number, with a projected cost for the year of $13,000. In buying the ad, I expected to get good quality leads that were looking for me. The day the new phone book came out I was so excited, especially when my phone started ringing; however, not one caller was looking to buy a house. They all wanted to order pizza. I paid the first month's charge of over $1,100, hoping things would change, but they did not. Another month went by and another hundred attempted orders for pizza came in. I called the rep complaining, but he reminded me I had signed a contract. I argued with him for several minutes. He told me the pizza company was no longer on the program. Need we wonder why? I told him he would be hearing from my attorney. He stammered for a moment and said, "Well, you do know that if we cut this number off, you won't get any more calls?" Exactly! Now there is real wisdom for you. I am able to laugh at the insanity of that conversation now. In sharing this story recently with an old college friend, he said, "You should have opened a pizza parlor." Believe me, the thought did cross my mind.

Many couples today find themselves having insane conversations without laughter. They don't laugh with each other. They don't laugh when they are in counseling. They don't even smile when they think about each other. Unfortunately, for many of these couples, one of the primary problems is their finances. They have a lot of "stuff," however, these material possessions ironically are the very reason they no longer have any esteem for each other.

Many couples today are being crushed by the reality of Proverbs 22:7: "the borrower is slave to the lender." The desire for riches and the illusion of success has put a wedge in the marriage that God never intended. Fights escalate; words are spoken that can't be taken back even when they are forgiven; thoughts begin to form that, if spoken, would absolutely destroy. I'm reminded again of the man who killed his wife on their wedding day over a prenuptial agreement (or disagreement). Even when a couple recognizes that a problem exists and they want to resolve it, they often have no idea how to best tackle it. One says, "We need to trust God. We should start tithing." The other says, "I trust God, but I'm not going to tithe." I know. We've been there. Sherry wanted to trust; I wanted to keep.

After the housing market crashed, I was called to pastor a church and accepted; it was not a good fit. The last six months we were there, Sherry would go to bed crying every night. We lasted eighteen months before I resigned on our twenty-fourth wedding anniversary. We moved back into a home that had never sold, while I began looking for a job. We had gone six months without any income or insurance when our third son was injured in a fire and had to be air-lifted to a hospital in Atlanta. The helicopter flight alone was over $20,000. The medical bills bankrupted us.

My faith was greatly tested at that time and I didn't want to tithe. I didn't feel that it was a possibility, even after I did gain employment at approximately a third of what I used to make as a broker. Sherry was embarrassed; she didn't want anyone to know. She felt absolutely humiliated sitting in the bankruptcy court and when our old church family gave us groceries. I felt like a complete failure—no more good name for me.

One thing Sherry didn't do was to stop praying. Me, I was too numb to pray. I still loved God, but I just didn't know how to pray anymore. I am very thankful that Sherry did not stop. As a result of her prayers, she sensed that God would have us to continue tithing. I tried to call her legalistic, but I know now that she wasn't concerned with following some set of rules. I knew so then, but in my fear and anger, I was not willing to admit that truth. Sherry, on the other hand, faced her fears with prayer, running to the only One who could save her, save us.

A white wicker chair sits on our front porch. That chair is a sacred place in my heart today, a place where Sherry sits to be alone with God. When she is there, I flip on the do not disturb button. I don't do so because she has asked me to, but because I know she is engaged in an incredible, private dialogue with God, from which great blessing flows for her and all of us around her. She has prayed us through numerous storms, including many involving our boys.

Not long ago, I saw a book on the bed stand on Sherry's side of the bed, *The Power of a Praying Wife* by Stormie Omartian. I've never met the author, but I can attest that such power is real. Earning a doctorate degree and completing a two-hundred-fifty-page dissertation on prayer and devotion did not benefit me as much as witnessing the power of a praying wife firsthand. A wife who loves the Lord is a mighty force that can transform the heart of a man.

Perhaps you are struggling over the idea of seeking God's solutions to your problems. Maybe you have this idea that you can resolve your difficulties on your own. Why would you want to act alone? Why do you keep trying to make a good name in your own power when God has given us everything we need to make it through His?

Tithing is just one demonstration of how His power flows through us when we believe and apply the principles of wisdom given to us in the Bible. Proverbs 22:9 tells us, "The generous will themselves be blessed ..." In prioritizing what's important in life, the heart is at the top of the list; money is much further down. Are we willing to take God at His word? The foundation of tithing is a generous heart, not a legalistic adherence to a dictate from God. I stand firmly against the legalism of tithing, but I boldly declare the blessing and joy of the act. If you tithe without joy, you likely do not experience joy in other areas of your life. As we learned in Proverbs 4, the issues of life flow out of the heart. Viewing our giving to God as a privilege and a blessing instead of a chore and near-impossible challenge is key in helping us to develop a good name.

If the idea of tithing is new to you, give it some thought. It's the one area in our lives where God specifically encourages us to test His faithfulness. Malachi 3:10 says, "'Test me in this,' says the Lord Almighty, 'and see if I will not throw open the floodgates of heaven and pour out so much blessing that there will not be room enough to store it.'" Over the years I have come to realize the true cost of giving is receiving. My faith has at times been challenged but has always been strengthened in the ways I have seen God provide when I have stepped out in faith trusting in His promises.

Couple Activity

- In what ways has your heritage (name) been a blessing or a curse? How might you benefit from developing a good name? How will you seek to implement the Proverbs 22:9 verse in your marriage and faith community?
- Name some ways you have been blessed by giving. Reflect upon how God blesses you as you give with a joyful heart.

Day 23

When Is Enough, Enough?

Do not wear yourself out to get rich;
do not trust your own cleverness.
—Proverbs 23:4

I was just sitting down to Thanksgiving dinner when the phone rang. The middle-aged couple said they were in town for a couple of days and wanted to see a house I had listed. "Super, I'll be glad to show it to you tomorrow morning."

"*No*, we're sitting in the driveway, and we want to see it right now. If you want to sell it, we'll see it *now*."

I didn't say it, but I did think, "If you really want to buy this house, it can wait till morning." Her tone told me these weren't the type of people I really wanted to do business with, but I responded to a sense of duty and told her I would be there in fifteen minutes. I pushed back from the table and received an incredulous look from Sherry. Fifteen minutes later, I was walking around the house with the two orneriest people I've ever met. Thankfully the seller was out of town visiting family. They saw nothing good about the house, even though the home was immaculately staged. Thirty minutes later they did say, "Thank you, but this won't do." I didn't offer my card. What a total waste of time. I made the decision that day to be more assertive in responding to unreasonable requests (especially when they cause me to miss out on Grandma's magic crust pie).

Growing up in East Point, Georgia, I especially enjoyed family outings to Hapeville to eat at the Dwarf House. When the first mall Chick-fil-A opened, I would ride my bike to Greenbriar Mall just to have a Chick-fil-A sandwich. I never went on Sundays, of course, because they were always closed. The company website states the reason: "Founder Truett Cathy made the decision to close on Sundays in 1946 when he opened his first restaurant. He has often shared that his decision was as much practical as spiritual. He believes that all franchised Chick-fil-A operators and their employees should have an opportunity to rest, spend time with family and friends, and worship if they choose to do so." I wish I had held the same philosophy on that Thanksgiving Day twenty years ago.

In one of his recent books, Mr. Cathy raised a question that many have pondered. *Wealth, is it worth it?* This question is interesting coming from such a wealthy man. Thankfully Mr. Cathy left a legacy of faith and integrity in using the blessings God gave him to bless others. For some men, wealth *is* worth it. Mr. Cathy was one of them. In my mind, I imagine the words he must have heard on September 8, 2014, just a few weeks ago, "Well done, good and faithful servant."

Mr. Cathy recognized two important truths about money: Wealth should be your servant and not the reverse; and you are simply a caretaker of that which is God's. Alternately, many have become servants to wealth to their own downfall. Wealth can be a dangerous thing. In the pursuit of it, many have lost their good name, their family, their freedom, and even their lives. Are you living your life in light of the first words you will hear when this life is over, or will you be one who says, "Oops"?

In 1999, a student in my appraisal school stole my professional identity. Two years later, I began receiving phone calls from banks wanting to know why I had overvalued some homes by more than $100,000. I had no idea what they were talking about and had never been in the cities where those homes were located. I reported what I thought were two or three cases of fraud to the appropriate authorities, only to find out that I was under investigation for $20 million in mortgage fraud—at the time, it was the largest mortgage scam in Georgia history. My name was placed on the government's *Don't Use* list, circulated to the various banks with which we did business. The consequences of making this notorious list included the destruction of one-third of my real estate organization.

As the investigation proceeded, investigators learned that I was not involved, so I was exonerated; however, neither my fears nor the fears of our bank clients were calmed. The perpetrators were not yet in jail. Furthermore, I had been subpoenaed to testify before the grand jury in a $20,000,000 fraud scheme. I knew that bad guys kill people for a whole lot less than this amount. I have never fought in a war like many of the soldiers I counsel, but I do understand the effects of trauma, at least to some degree. I began carrying a pistol and was afraid for my children to be home alone. I was nervous about showing houses to people I didn't know. In restaurants, I sat where I could see everyone who entered. During this time, I also began questioning everything I thought was important. Eventually I would know the answers, but not until after a few more trials in life. These circumstances almost made me believe that my years of training my sons to be men of God was really for my own sake rather than theirs.

Criminology professor Dennis Stevens wrote about the case in 2011 in his book *Wicked Women, A Journey of Super Predators.* Thankfully my name is not in the book, but fourteen others are. Thirteen individuals turned state's evidence and received seven-year sentences. The ring leader received a thirty-year mandatory sentence for federal racketeering.

I learned much about the importance of forgiveness from that experience. Seeing those criminals get what they deserved was not enough to give me peace. If I failed to forgive, I too would be in a prison, one of my own making. I would be a "dead man walking." I have a deep appreciation for the story of Joseph in Genesis 50. His brothers turned on him and sold him into slavery, yet he eventually overcame his circumstances to be named second-in-command over all of Egypt. Years later during a time of famine, he saved his family when they came searching for food. I have not seen those broken individuals who wronged me since the day they were sentenced, but if I did, I would say to them what Joseph said to his brothers, "You intended to harm me, but God intended it for good to accomplish what is now being done, the saving of many lives." I know I would not be doing what I now do had it not been for the trials I have seen. I have shared my story to ask you a question.

What are you striving for? When is enough, enough? Sure, you have to make a living. I get that, but has all your striving really brought you the joy you thought it would bring? Are you staying in a job you hate just because it brings home the bacon? My friend Bob Buford writes in his book *Half Time,* "We have to be careful with the idea that the object of work is to earn enough money so that we can someday quit working and live a life of leisure. Leisure is an occasional gift we need to give ourselves, but full-time leisure, as appealing as it may sound, is simply not good for your mental or emotional health. It never works."

When I stepped away from a corporate job in 2013 to serve full-time for a start-up nonprofit, more than a few folks raised their eyebrows. "Are you crazy? In this economy? Really?" My income is a third of what it was during the so-called good times, but I have never felt greater joy. I have had the privilege over the past few years of working with more than twenty-four thousand soldiers and have seen many lives transformed, beginning with mine. My path hasn't been easy, but then I wasn't looking for easy. Rather, my goal was, as Bob says, to "move from success to significance."

Is what you are doing easy? Are you lacking peace as you worry over bills and struggle with the stress of thinking you must have it all? I'm not certain of the reasons—whether thought patterns change sometime around the age of fifty or my experiences have had a particular impact on me, but when I hit this age, I realized that I have only so many kilowatts of life left in me. I have only so many days, hours, minutes, and seconds left. I refuse to burn any more kilowatts on those things that just don't matter. One day the lights *will* go out; the next chapter of eternity will begin. What preparation are you making for that day? When is enough, enough?

Couple Activity

- What does "enough" look like to you?
- Is your attitude, "I earned it; I'll keep it" or "God gave it; I'll give it"?
- What do your answers to these questions reveal about your character and faith?
- What changes, if any, do you need to make in your priorities and values in order to live a more peaceful, Christ-centered life?

Day 24

Filling Your Home with Beauty

By wisdom a house is built ... through knowledge its
rooms are filled with rare and beautiful treasures.
—Proverbs 24:2–4

I've been a licensed real estate agent since 1986. In that time, I have seen many beautiful homes. In my mind I can see a big fuzzy picture of some of them. Yet I am hard pressed at the moment to recall the details of any of them except for one. It was unlike any other home that I ever sold. In fact, I didn't sell it. The owners were not my clients. They were my great aunt and uncle. The home itself was a modest three-bedroom with nothing in itself that makes it stand out, and yet I can vividly recall the details. It was a brick home with window-unit air conditioning, a big picture window in the living room, a small kitchen, and a phone on the wall that had the longest cord I had ever seen. I remember picking apples and playing hide and seek with my sister and cousins. I would hide in a drainage ditch in the front yard near the street. It's almost a Narnia-like experience as I think of it now. All the other homes fade in my memory, but this one remains.

It was not beautiful because of the things inside of it but because of the people who lived there: "Through knowledge its rooms were filled with rare and beautiful treasures" (Proverbs 24:4). Uncle Zack was a quiet man. Their daughter (my cousin) told me that every night her dad would get on his knees and pray before bed. My aunt Willie Lee was a woman full of wisdom. As I got older, I wasn't able to visit her as much as I had done as a child, but I still called her. She was always such an encouragement to me and loved me like I was her own son. Many times she would literally sing to me over the phone.

We have covered a lot of ground since we first began this journey together. Hopefully there is a sense of progression. On day 9, we considered that we must be careful of those we invite into our homes and our lives as we learn to walk in wisdom. We have also considered the importance of the family name, finances, and how to avoid strife. In the coming days we will consider those things that will help us when we are weary, the importance of not only having a mentor but becoming one, and finally the greatest blessing that God gives a man.

There are many things that we can acquire in life, but none is more valuable than a home that is built with wisdom. Such a home is one that little children will fondly remember when they are old, and those who dwelt there will be remembered when they are long gone.

Recently Sherry and I were visiting with friends Jack and Roy Ann Smith. I asked them what the key has been for them during their sixty years of marriage. Jack said, "Thirty-five or forty years ago, someone asked Roy Ann that very question. Her one word was 'commitment.' I can't improve on that. It is the perfect answer. On October 9, 1954, both of us made a vow (commitment) to each other and to God. For me to go back on that commitment would be an insult to God, Roy Ann, and to myself."

Roy Ann followed up, "Staying married for sixty years not only takes commitment to our sacred vows before God but also takes love. To keep love alive, each year we take a trip to commemorate our wedding date. Each day, Jack and I say to each other, 'I love you.' On our honeymoon we drove on Route 66. Now, when we hear that song, we are filled with memories of our honeymoon. Love takes constant polishing to keep it shiny and glowing." Both Sherry and I sensed that Jack and Roy Ann are genuinely happy. After dinner, Sherry and I watched as they walked to their car hand in hand.

In the appraisal division of our company we would annually appraise more than $250 million in homes, but you can't put a price on a happy home filled with wisdom. Such a home really is a beautiful treasure. If the old African proverb is true that, "It takes a village to raise a child," then couples do well too to glean from the collective wisdom of the community. Couples sometimes need the encouragement of others to help them understand that they are not alone in the challenge of strengthening marriage. Sherry and I have gleaned much wisdom from dear friends who willingly share their lives with us. Having a strong network of two to three couples is a tremendous source of encouragement in building marriage resilience and building a happy home. So today, I simply want to share with you a few insights Sherry and I have learned from some of our dear friends.

Rick was my college roommate thirty years ago. He and Heather have been married since 1995. For them, "marriage is not a fifty-fifty business arrangement. It's a union before God where there will be times you give 80 percent and times you will give 20 percent, but yoked together, it will always add up to 100 percent. There will be times you willingly give more and times you give more because it's necessary, but if you remember you're here to serve one another, your time together will be sweet, and your percentage won't matter because you're together."

Debbie and Adrien Neely met on *eHarmony* and have been married since 2004. The key for them is that "neither feels a need to have to always be right. Always look for ways to keep peace in the family. Honor your spouse. Make it a win-win marriage!"

Jim and Irene Murphy have been married since 1966 and have been dear friends in my life for more than forty-five years. Irene wrote me the other day: "Each day we have our own quiet time with the Lord, but at breakfast we have our family devotions. We did this when our children were small and continue devotions until this day. Never go to sleep at night or go out of the house to run an errand without a kiss and an 'I love you!' If one or the other isn't at home, leave a note as to where you are and when to expect you back home. Leave sweet notes under the pillow if you are going to be away for several days. Always remember birthdays and anniversaries with a card and maybe a gift. Discuss issues that may annoy you with your spouse. Do it in a kind, gentle manner without raising voices. Buy two tubes of toothpaste. One may be a middle-squeezer and the other from the bottom. Thank goodness we roll the toilet tissue the same way."

Sherry and I have fond memories of staying with Jim and Irene twenty years ago, and yes, they had family devotion time at the breakfast table. Irene, I still struggle with the toilet paper thing.

My friend, Dr. James Thomas, pastors the church that ordained me into the ministry in 1989. He and his bride Laura have been married since 1995. He says, "Marriage is hard work, and it is spiritual work. Though many don't necessarily relate the hard work of marriage to their walk with Christ, Jesus intentionally utilized the marriage relationship as an illustration of His love for the Church (Ephesians 6:25–33). Marriage, therefore, becomes a visible manifestation of Christ's love."

Gerald and Martha Jean Harris have been married since 1963. Gerald points out a subject that we have not considered but needs to be understood as we seek to grow in wisdom: "In a healthy marriage all three kinds of love are important. 'Eros' is like a spark plug in an automobile. It's not as important as the engine, but the spark plug ignites the fire that gets the engine going. A romantic love keeps the emotions charged with life and light. 'Phileo' is a kind of love that binds a husband and wife together as friends. 'Agape' is that spiritual love that exists when the bride and groom are followers of Jesus Christ. It is that 'agape' love that will hold a marriage together in the storms and trials of life."

Jamie and Doug Pyles have been married since 1979. Jamie says, "One of the greatest lessons to learn early on is about assumptions. They can make or break a marriage or really any relationship! If you always assume the best motives of the other, you are on your way to a great relationship, but *all* negative assumptions should be shared with the other and allowed to be clarified. Otherwise, it can mean slow death to any relationship."

Sitting around the kitchen table, Sherry and I enjoyed fresh fried apple pie and ice cream with Barney and Sue Walker. Recently the

Walkers celebrated sixty-three years of marriage. Sue said, "We gave each other room to do the things we liked to do individually. We never said harsh words that we couldn't take back; to protect our marriage we would nip things in the bud that could be a problem down the road; and we both had praying moms." Barney said, "Marriage is a partnership. Just as in business, so in marriage be fair, practice good ethics, and pay your debts. These things help make marriage stronger. One thing I learned early on is that if what you're doing is so loud that she can't hear what you're saying, you have a problem" Sue did say when they first started dating she was so impressed that Barney brought her chocolate-covered cherries while she was in the hospital. "But the doubts came quickly as he sat there and ate almost every single one." We enjoyed some good laughs with the Walkers. The last thing Sue considered a high priority is to, "always remember important dates."

Finally, my pastor, Keith Moore who has been married to Allison since 1973 shares, "Everyone needs someone who thinks they hung the moon. Treat your spouse like you believe they are that person! Never have fun at the expense of your spouse. Never criticize or make fun of your spouse in public. Many couples do this as a lifestyle, and it is always destructive. No matter how funny it is, your spouse feels like it is thinly veiled hostility. Most of the time, he or she is correct." Pastor, I have told Sherry now several times, "I think you hung the moon." It not only tickles her, but it makes me feel good to say it. Thanks for the tip.

I greatly appreciate these friends allowing me to share with you the insights that have blessed their marriages. All total, these couples represent almost four hundred years of marriage wisdom. Thanks guys!

As a real estate broker of almost thirty years, I have observed many times a correlation between the things of life that are beyond our financial reach and the health of marriages. Regardless of age, couples that buy the biggest house they can possibly afford and fill it with the financed treasures of apparent success do not seem nearly as happy as those who demonstrate temperance. This observation does beg the question, "Is the financial strain of having to have it all the cause or the symptom of a troubled marriage?" Some would say it is the cause. I tend to think it is the symptom.

Certainly poor financial decisions can further weaken a troubled marriage; and even the best of marriages can be tested by unexpected life events. However, a healthy marriage established by the principles of wisdom allows each partner to better withstand the inevitable stresses of life. When we understand that the greatest treasures of the home are the relationships within, we are less inclined to fill the void with those things that can never truly fill the void. Wisdom fills the rooms of your home with rare and beautiful treasure. It also fills the heart and helps you come to the knowledge that a beautiful relationship is the key to the most joyous home you can imagine.

Couple Activity

- Identify in your relationship what your real treasures are.
- How much value do you put on that treasure?
- What will you do to enhance the value of your treasure?
- What are the tangible benefits of valuing the true treasure?

Day 25

When You Are Weary

Like cold water to a weary soul
is good news from a distant land.
—Proverbs 25:25

On day 11, we considered the importance of looking for the good, while on day 14 we talked about building goodwill. Honestly, carrying out these goals can be hard sometimes. Just yesterday a call from my insurance company announced that a suit was being brought for the accident my son was involved in. On first glance, I might be tempted to think that all our attempts at goodwill were in vain. However, I have this overwhelming sense of peace, perhaps because of the goodwill I have sought to have with the heavenly Father in seeking His wisdom to write this book. I hung up the phone, and immediately Proverbs 3:5–6 popped into my head: "Trust in the Lord with all your heart and lean not on your own understanding; in all your ways submit to him, and he will make your paths straight." If we hide God's Word in our hearts for no other reason than to recall it when bad things happen, then we are still greatly blessed.

Sometimes it does seem like the cards are stacked against us. We may grow weary in our individual lives and in marriage as well. Bad news seems to be all around. I rarely watch the news nowadays for that very reason. The other night I did watch, just to see if an observation I had heard is true. The idea is that for every story reported about positive events, seventeen stories about negative events are presented. Sure enough, in the one hour I sat there watching, I saw only one good, heartwarming story. Everything else was bad. Little wonder that we are so stressed out. Bad news actually causes the body to release stress hormones into our bloodstream. In my work with wounded soldiers, I am very much aware of the physical changes that occur within the prefrontal cortex of the brain in soldiers suffering from PTSD. The wiring of the brain is actually scrambled, making it virtually impossible to have one rational, positive thought. I'll admit that for a split-second after that phone call from the insurance company, I had flashbacks to the $20 million lawsuit that had stressed my life to the breaking point a dozen years earlier. In bringing the situation to the light of God's Word, the fear was instantly vanquished.

I am working with a man right now who is extremely weary. He seems to be in a rut that he can't shake. Things are bad at home and bad at work. The young bucks in the office treat him like he is incompetent, while he feels his wife treats him much the same at home. For sure, he has a challenge before him, but his situation won't get better if he continues to focus on the negative. Changing his mind-set may be very difficult, but doing so is imperative.

I had a soldier tell me that he couldn't run the two-mile army PT test. I certainly sympathize; I hate running, myself. As a power lifter, running has never been my forte. Push-ups and sit-ups are a cakewalk, but running—well, let's just say I deplore it with every fast-twitch fiber of my being. Like this soldier, though, I have to complete the run in the required time if I want to stay in the army, so I gave him the same challenge I had given myself. I asked him, "Can you run one hundred yards?"

"Yes, sir."

"Okay, just run one hundred yards today. Don't focus on what you can't do. Focus on what you can do. You can run one hundred yards. Tomorrow, add another fifty yards to it. Can you do that?"

"Yes, sir."

"Private, do you realize if you will just add fifty yards, one hundred fifty feet, to every run, in seventy days you will be running two miles?"

"Yes, sir, but I'm not good at math."

"I'm not talking about math, Private. I'm talking about running. Oh, and by the way, you get to rest every other day. At that pace, you will be ready in four months for that PT test that is six months away."

I know—all the runners out there have got a better plan, but don't miss the point. It's not about what you can't do; it's about what you can do. My Bible tells me, "I can do all things through Him who gives me strength" (Philippians 4:13). When the boys were little, we had a family motto in our home: "We are the can-do Koons!" It's a belief that my mom and dad taught me.

In my army reserve unit, I work with 7000 soldiers spread across the USA from Camp Parks, California, to Fort Dix, New Jersey. The counseling I give them "is good news from a distant land." (Proverbs 25:25) Many men who are anchors in my life are men who live far away, but I call them often when I need cold water for my weary soul. We'll talk more on day 27 about finding and being a mentor; for now, simply understand the importance of surrounding yourself with individuals who strengthen your spirit when you are down. Iron sharpens iron.

We live in a world of bad news. With the growth of the Internet, our world is much smaller. We hear of things now in a nanosecond and, for whatever reason, love bad news. History reminds us that we are often slow to hear good news. Lieutenant Hiroo Onoda of the Imperial Japanese Army continued to hide out and evade search parties for thirty years after World War II ended. He thought the leaflets dropped from airplanes declaring the war to be over were a trick of the enemy. Many other soldiers from this war and others continued to fight without reason.

Sadly many couples are the same. She refuses to believe that he is really trying. All he can hear is her "nagging." The positive affirmations of love and respect are virtually nonexistent. The letters from God have been dropped from heaven, but the negative thoughts tell them both it's a trick, that the positive words from Scripture don't apply to them, so the battle rages on.

Given the option, would you prefer to continue fighting for the next thirty years or experience victory, a *win-win victory* for your marriage? If you choose the former, then one of us is missing something ... and I don't think it's me.

The cold water for your weary soul is this: You can have a victorious marriage. You can't do it by continuing to behave as you always have. Some things have to change. You've probably heard this notion before within your marriage. The starting point of change is in your mind and is motivated by the desires of your heart. If in your heart, you truly desire to have a victorious marriage, then you must train your mind to dwell on those things that will enable that victory. Do you recall the reference to Paul's words on day 15? You must have noble, right, pure, lovely, admirable, excellent, and praiseworthy thoughts toward each other.

You may believe that having such thoughts within your marriage would be like trying to run a three-legged, two-mile PT test when you can't do ten yards together without falling. You are going to fall occasionally, but remember that you are not running in your own strength. God, through Christ and through the wisdom of His Word, gives you everything you need. He wants to give you the very mind of Christ. Your responsibility is to believe so and act upon what He reveals through the wisdom He imparts.

Joining in work toward common goals, helping around the house, speaking softly, and fighting fairly will relieve much of the stress that is often self-induced or spouse-induced and infuse energy into the marriage in more ways than one. Let's face it, when she is feeling overwhelmed and weary because the house is always a wreck, no matter her efforts to clean, she will not put forth much effort to consider your physical relationship, which can greatly bless the marriage. Can you really blame her? She's worn out being the maid, cook, janitor, school master, taxi driver, and everything else that keeps the household running.

I know you both have been weary at times, maybe even most of the time. You may feel like that soldier who couldn't run two miles even though his job counted on it. I also know you want the marriage that you had in your mind when you said "I do." You can't do two miles? No sweat. Are you willing to do fifty yards? Good, let's get started. Tomorrow we'll do another fifty!

Couple Activity

- Ask each other the following: What is the one thing you would like to hear from me that I believe about you?
- If you struggle in your answer, say it anyway, with all the sincerity you can muster.
- Anchor that thought in your heart and mind as if it is cold water for a weary soul. It will be a blessing to you as well.

Day 26

Putting Out Fires

Without wood a fire goes out …
—Proverbs 26:20

Without deep thought, the reader can interpret Proverbs 26 as negative, harsh, and at times contradictory. Honestly, my first thought was, "We'll just skip over it!" I've often been accused of being a bit of a Pollyanna, irrationally optimistic. I like being around positive people and struggle with the negativity that seems to constantly flow out of some people. At first glance, chapter 26 is rather depressing; however, since I believe that every word in the Bible is inspired by God, I knew I had to keep digging.

As I read through Proverbs 26, I couldn't help but think of several men I have known who walked away from their marriages. Afterward, I could see that in their hearts they harbored deceit, as Proverbs 26:24 describes. Their flattery and charm was full of lies. They may have concealed their deception for a while, but an astute person could discern their true nature over time. I sold a house to a couple several years ago. He said they needed a one-story home because his wife was ill and could no longer maneuver two stories. Shortly after closing, he delivered divorce papers to her as she lay in a hospital bed on Valentine's Day. I served as interim pastor in a church where the pastor had stepped down to take another job. He took the job to be close to his mistress. In another case, a man even had the nerve to ask his estranged wife if she would go on vacation with him and his mistress so that she could watch the kids. I could go on, but you get the picture.

In each of these situations and many similar ones, I tried to reach out to these men, but they would not have it. I haven't seen any of those men since, but every so often I do see their former wives. Thankfully they have worked through the pain and continue to do so. They have not been destroyed by the crushing blows inflicted upon them. Through much prayer and support from others who surrounded them with love, these women are overcoming and experiencing the power of God's love in the midst of their pain. Even though these men tried to "work ruin," God is bigger and stronger than a foolish man. No doubt, many women have also walked away from their marriages, but I can't help but wonder what role the man had in their decisions. The man or woman who is wise will not be undone simply because they married a foolish person.

The apostle Paul tells us in 1 Corinthians 10:13, "No temptation has overtaken you except what is common to mankind. And God is faithful; he will not let you be tempted beyond what you can bear. But when you are tempted, he will also provide a way out so that you can endure it." Once, a man quoted that verse to me, leaving out the last six words. He wasn't looking to endure; he wanted out.

Just because you married a foolish person doesn't mean you have to stoop to their level and act like a fool yourself. Neither does it mean that divorce is inevitable. Sometimes you are called to endure, while at other times, you see a foolish person in your life reach such an overwhelming sense of brokenness that he or she repents of his or her foolish ways and turns to God for salvation. Such a situation is the essence of the gospel. Until we come to Christ, we are all fools: "The fool says in his heart, 'There is no God.' They are corrupt, their deeds are vile; there is no one who does good" (Psalm 14:1).

If you are living with a foolish spouse, the book of Proverbs is filled with instructions that provide a way to endure. But nonbelievers have often used verses 4 and 5 of Proverbs 26 to prove the Bible contradicts itself. Verse 4 reads, "Do not answer a fool according to his folly, or you yourself will be just like him." Verse 5 reads, "Answer a fool according to his folly, or he will be wise in his own eyes." We read these verses and wonder what the correct course of action is. An apparent contradiction does exist.

Proverbs 26:20 sheds further light and is a call for greater wisdom: "Without wood a fire goes out." In other words, don't give a foolish spouse ammunition by being foolish yourself. When we fight the way they fight, we lose. Remember—the wise person doesn't fight against a spouse but for the marriage. Fighting like a fool with a fool is fighting against the marriage. Sometimes our best course of action is not to give an answer. However, surely if we do give one, we should do so in a gentle way (as Proverbs 15:1 tells us). Our goal should not be to prove a point or to further an argument. In matters of personal opinion Proverbs 26:4 would likely apply. Don't waste your time and energy arguing with others on matters of personal opinion. If you do, you will be arguing all the time since everybody has an opinion. Times of disagreement call for much wisdom and should encourage us to live our lives according to the advice in 2 Timothy 2:15, "Do your best to present yourself to God as one approved, a worker who does not need to be ashamed and who correctly handles the word of truth."

Obviously we will sometimes have to give a response when opinions do vary. Proverbs 26:5 instructs us regarding those occasions. When the words of the foolish person might lead others astray, or your silence might cause you to appear complicit, it's time to speak up. We are a nation on the brink of destruction today in large part because the majority of citizens will not speak up for the truth. As Edmund Burke said more than 250 years ago, "All that is necessary for the triumph of evil is that good men do nothing." Sometimes this adage applies in marriage as well. Sometimes we have to speak up!

For several summers during college, I worked on the ramp at the Atlanta airport. Another employee would often curse and rant in the break room. I suffered through this negativity until he took God's name in vain. Then, I spoke up and firmly told him that his words were offensive to me, and that I would appreciate his not speaking such words in my presence. I never heard him say another foul word. Another time, a friend and I were unloading a plane for another team so that they could eat lunch. The team lead came out and said, "You don't need to be doing this. You're making us look bad." Our team was sitting in the break room smoking and chatting. My friend responded, "Frank Borman may sign our checks, but we work for a Jewish carpenter." The lead walked off with his head hanging; however, the next day the lead was handing out evangelistic tracts and inviting people to his church. Sometimes foolishness can be corrected. Wisdom will know when those opportunities lie before us.

Couple Activity

- How will you differentiate between the important (essential) arguments and those that are a matter of personal opinion?
- What are some ways that you and your spouse can guard your hearts against deceit?

Day 27

Find a Mentor—Be a Mentor

As iron sharpens iron, so one person sharpens another.
—Proverbs 27:17

I have been blessed to have some great mentors in my life. My dad was one of them; however, he died when I was just reaching the *age of realization,* which I view as similar to the *age of accountability.* Neither of these phrases is specifically explained in the Bible, but I think both hold great importance, as I will explain.

Two-year-olds have a certain level of accountability, but ten-year-olds have more. In the same way, a marriage of thirty years hopefully has more maturity in it than one of two years. Before I was married, a friend asked me to be in his wedding. I refused to do so, because, like everyone else, I could see that the marriage was the attempt of two teenagers to escape difficult family situations. The marriage lasted less than a year. As we mature, hopefully we come to a greater understanding of the difference between right and wrong. The love chapter, 1 Corinthians 13:11, puts it this way: "When I was a child, I talked like a child, I thought like a child, I reasoned like a child. When I became a man, I put the ways of childhood behind me."

The age of realization for a man, or at least my intended definition of it, is that moment in time when you realize that your parents did know what they were talking about after all, and that you're not as smart as you thought you were. For most men, it usually hits them many years after the age of accountability—at least it did in my case. I had just celebrated my twenty-seventh birthday and was standing by my dad's bedside as he breathed his last breath. That's when it hit me. Many times over the years since then, I have wished that I could pick up the phone and talk to Dad.

Because I missed out on those opportunities, I have been very intentional in developing close relationships with my sons. Like me, they too went through some fairly difficult prerealization struggles; in many ways they continue to do so. One night I was sitting out by the fire pit with my oldest son, MaCrae. He had recently asked Lauren to be his bride. In the shadows of the fire, I hid the tears welling up in my eyes as he began to share his heart. One of his revelations was that he had been praying his brothers would understand that his mom and dad have some things to offer that can save them much grief if they will only consider the words we share. I couldn't help but think of Proverbs 27:11 as he spoke: "Be wise, my son, and bring joy to my heart."

Ken Jones has been both a dear friend and mentor in my life for more than thirty years. To this day, he continues to impact the lives of college students as the campus minister at the University of North Georgia. I will admit that he had some things to say to me when I was a college student that I didn't want to hear, but he loved me enough to say them anyway. For iron to sharpen iron, a rub must occur. "Wounds from a friend can be trusted," Proverbs 27:6 tells us. Some people say, "Oh that person just rubs me the wrong way" but don't realize that situation is actually very positive. Hopefully with wisdom, they will learn to know better.

Ken taught me the importance of keeping Christ at the center of relationships in my dating life. When I finally understood what he was saying, he made me the prayer coordinator for the student ministry organization. I took to the role with great passion and will confess a somewhat ulterior motive. In a female-dominated organization, I was able to pick a cute little blonde to be my prayer partner. On our first scheduled prayer time together, I took her to the Chestatee River that flows through Dahlonega, Georgia. We talked for a few minutes about school and family. Then, I asked her if she wanted to start or if I should. I'm not sure exactly what she was thinking, but it wasn't about prayer. When I reminded her that we needed to pray, I could see the immediate disconnection in her eyes. That loving feeling was gone. She couldn't believe I was serious. Her reaction reminds me of a lot of church prayer meetings I have attended. In our case, I was determined that we were going to pray. The next week she conveniently had other plans, so I moved on to the next coed.

You can imagine how I felt a few years later, when I took Sherry out for the first time. We didn't know each other, but before we headed to dinner she asked if I would say a prayer before we left her house. When I got home a few hours later, Mom asked how the date went. I told her I was going to marry that girl. Two months later, we were engaged. I have four people to thank for my marriage: Mom for telling me about Sherry, Ken for teaching me how to treat her, Sherry for saying yes, and God for blessing it these twenty-nine years. Don't wake me if I am dreaming!

I have passed on the lessons I learned from Ken to many of the twenty-five thousand soldiers I have worked with in the past four years. That's the power of a mentor—he makes other mentors. He pours truth into the lives of others who touch people he will never know. A great mentor produces mentors.

Till our last breath, we will have trials in this life. I've stood by enough bedsides to know this truth and see it even now in the life of one of my family members as she lovingly takes care of her husband who has Alzheimer's disease. I also see devastating trials in the lives of many men who bring trials upon themselves because of lack of wisdom. I was saddened recently to hear of yet another pastor who had to step down from his pulpit because of infidelity. Obviously he is accountable for his actions, but I wonder if he had anyone in his life—not just deacons, but someone in his life that was willing to ask tough questions and hold him accountable to his calling, not only as a pastor but as a man of God and a husband.

I remember well a beautiful spring day thirty years ago when I was relaxing by the school pool instead of attending a scheduled student ministry council meeting. Ken walked up to me with tears in his eyes and firmly reminded me that I have responsibilities. He talked to me about my identity. He held me accountable to a higher standard. A couple of summers ago, I had the privilege of teaching the Identity Seminar to his students in Panama City, Florida. The session simply consisted of lessons I had learned about identity, largely because Ken, my college mentor had been willing to hold me accountable to my true identity. Ken, it's time for another road trip to PC!

The greatest joy of a mentor is in producing other mentors. Luke 6:40 tells us, "The student is not above the teacher, but everyone who is fully trained will be like their teacher." My prayer for my sons has always been to have wisdom to pour into their lives so that one day they could pour that wisdom into others and that I would have the humility to receive wisdom from them as well.

Having those who are willing to work with you and walk with you to a place of maturity is an incredible blessing. This process takes great work, but if you are faithful, you will gain much reward. A well-trained mentee will become a well-trained mentor. James 1:4 says, "Let perseverance finish its work so that you may be mature and complete, not lacking anything." Wisdom will not only be a blessing to you, but it will flow through you as a blessing to others.

What does a mentor look like? He is mature and complete, lacking nothing. He will always be a student but also, at the same time, a teacher. He is never self-assured but rather is totally confident in God. In those times when he must wound, he does so with tears in his eyes and not a haughty, arrogant spirit. In those places where he lacks wisdom, he knows to seek it. Finally, when he sees a need for more wisdom in his own life, he believes that he will receive it.

> If any of you lacks wisdom, you should ask God, who gives generously to all without finding fault, and it will be given to you. But when you ask, you must believe and not doubt, because the one who doubts is like a wave of the sea, blown and tossed by the wind. That person should not expect to receive anything from the Lord. Such a person is double-minded and unstable in all they do. (James 1:5–8)

I have heard some men say they don't need a mentor. "I've got God on my side," they say. Some have even argued that having a mentor is not scriptural. I beg to differ. Joshua had Moses; Elisha had Elijah;

and Timothy had Paul, who reminded him "to fan into flame the gift of God, which is in you …" (2 Timothy 1:6). I know in my own life that the mentors I have had were a great blessing that helped bring more stability to my life and marriage.

A mentor is someone who believes in you and, more importantly, believes in God and what God wants to do in your life—especially when you find it hard to believe yourself. A good mentor is one who encourages you to keep pressing, to keep believing and to never give up. Though it has happened often in my life, I am still amazed that when I am seeking direction or sensing a lack of wisdom concerning something, I receive a well-timed call from a mentor who has just the words of wisdom or encouragement I need at the moment.

Whether you are newly married or have been married for years, you can greatly benefit from the wise counsel of others. After twenty-nine years of marriage, I continue to seek out men who can pour truth into my life. As a couple, Sherry and I have greatly benefited from the relationships of other couples who are living their lives according to principles of biblical wisdom. Some may not even realize the example they have been; they may have never considered themselves to be our mentors, but they were and still are. We are better for the wisdom that they've helped impart to our lives!

Couple Activity

- Who do you consider a potential mentor in your life?
- What will you do to foster such a relationship?
- In what ways will you seek to pass on the lessons you learn to others?

Day 28

What's the Chance of That?

Blessed is the one who always trembles before God,
but whoever hardens their heart falls into trouble.
—Proverbs 28:14

I have alluded to a particular issue throughout our time together, but I wouldn't be a very good battle buddy and would be remiss in my duties if I failed to address this next topic head on. I have deferred the bulk of this topic until now for two reasons. First, if I had come straight out of the chute on this matter, I would no doubt have lost a few of you from the start. Second, hopefully in prefacing with my own struggles and challenges in fully operating with wisdom in my life, you have seen clearly that I am simply a man prone to weakness like any other man. I am reminded of James's description of Elijah when he says "Elijah was a human being, even as we are" (James 5:17). At times he was filled with fear; he ran; he hid; and he even wanted to die. When he was weary from the battle, the Lord told him, "Get up." There was one more thing he needed to do.

As a husband, I am most ashamed of the day I attempted to introduce pornography into my marriage. We had been married less than a year.

What's even worse, I was a seminary student. Thankfully Sherry would not have anything to do with the filth. I can only imagine how my desire to do so crushed her spirit; I can't even comprehend the grace that had to be in her life because of her love from and for Jesus. Why would a beautiful young woman want to be married to a slug like me? It could only be grace.

Filled with fear, I was able to keep the temptation at bay for a season of time, but then the Internet came along. While the Internet has produced great wealth for some and in many ways made life easier, it has also destroyed many men and complicated their lives. A man no longer has to cope with that sleazy feeling he gets standing in front of the clerk at the local convenience store. The Internet offers him that feeling in the privacy of his *man cave* without even costing a dime.

In my work as a suicide intervention trainer, I know that pornography is a risk factor in developing suicidal ideation. In January 2014, a thirty-five-year-old senator's aide took his life after leaving a suicide note revealing that he had had an addiction to pornography. The rate of suicide among porn stars is substantially higher than other Hollywood celebrities. I believe that for the man who calls himself a Christian, the torment is even greater.

James 4:8–10 speaks of a double-minded man's need to grieve, mourn, and wail and ultimately to be purified and to humble himself before the Lord. Being caught in double-mindedness seems like a good recipe for mental illness. In my own life, I often felt like I was on the edge of that abyss. I wanted to do right, but I would cave in. I would experience that momentary high and just as quickly spiral into self-loathing. Repeatedly I would remind myself of Genesis 4:7: "If you do what is right, will you not be accepted? But if you do not do what is right, sin is crouching at your door; it desires to have you, but you must rule over it." I felt powerless to rule over my temptations; my sheer will and determination were not enough. Just as Cain acted on his temptations, so I opened the door.

Our proverb for today tells us that a man is "blessed who trembles before God." A man can also reach a point where he no longer fears God, which ironically turns out to be the most fearful place of all. His heart becomes hardened. He refuses to see the damage he is doing to his marriage and his very life. I saw myself moving in that direction. My only hope was to heed wisdom's call. I had to do things God's way. My way was no longer working.

One day Sherry and I went to preview a home that we were planning to list. As we spoke with the lady of the home, I sensed that she was a woman with a broken spirit. My observation did not have anything to do with what she said but was just a sense that something was not right. At the end of the tour, I realized what the problem was. The garage was his space, with walls covered in *Beer Babe* posters and nude centerfolds. What was the message these things shouted loud and clear? I think we know.

What I share with you now is not a formula for success. It's not a hidden secret I have uncovered because I'm some mystic seer who knows something you don't know; however, it is the most powerful force available to man in all the universe. If you will receive it, it *will* change your life. You must really want it, just like the lame man who wanted to be whole. It's just one word, but you must not only receive it—you must believe it with all your heart. Are you ready? Here's the one word: *Truth*!

Ken, you're telling me that "truth" will set me free? I didn't coin it; Jesus did. When he was speaking to the Jews who believed, he said, "Then you will know the truth and the truth will set you free" (John 8:32). When we receive the truth, we accept God's way of doing things. The things he calls us to do are not in our own power. We gain the ability and power to do them from the truth that is operating in our lives.

Ken, now you're telling me that if I let this concept or idea of truth work in my life, I will gain some kind of supernatural breakthrough that I have never had before? *Yes* and *no*. Yes, you will have a power that you have never had before. It will enable you to overcome every stronghold and live life to the fullest. It will transform your heart, your behaviors, and even your marriage. But *no*, it is not a concept; it's not an idea. It is not even an *it*. The power that will transform your life is a person; His name is Jesus. He said, "I am the way, the truth and the life" (John 14:6). When you believe Him and receive Him, it is His power that works in your life and changes your mind about who you are and who you were meant to be. He reveals how you have lived your life to this point and how it can be made new.

The power He makes available to you is the power of His Holy Spirit. His Spirit begins to work on your mind as you hear the *Truth* to bring your thoughts to Him. Paul said, "We take captive every thought to make it obedient to Christ" (2 Corinthians 10:5). The man who doesn't capture his thoughts will be captured *by* his thoughts; however, the one who brings his thoughts to Christ will be given the very mind of Christ. You will have a wisdom that is not of this world. The man without the Holy Spirit can never have the mind of Christ. He will continue to operate in his power and will fall into trouble, sooner or later.

The *Truth* also reveals that the lure of sin no longer has power over, us because of the greater power that is now in us. Does temptation no longer taunt us? No, it's always crouching at the door, but we are no longer fighting in our own power. We no longer have to cave in, in our *man cave*. The fastest way to crush future attacks is by bringing them to the light. Logically we grasp that darkness immediately disappears in the presence of light. When we continue to walk in darkness, we do so not because the light failed us but because we have denied the *Truth*, by failing to walk in the light.

One night I was trying to figure out a new smart phone. I didn't know how bright the flashlight app would be, so I flipped it on to see if Sherry was awake. "Hey, you awake?"

"Well, I am now." I looked around, and I didn't see any darkness in the room. Let that mental picture sink in for a second. What is darkness but the absence of light? It has no power and never has. It's nothing. All of hell's power is nothing in the light of God. Satan's lies about your identity, your sinfulness, the ways he twists God's promises, and all your broken promises are nothing in the light of *truth*. Charles Wesley's words come to mind: "He breaks the power of canceled sin, He sets the prisoner free; His blood can make the foulest clean, His blood availed for me." Paul told the Ephesians, "For you were once darkness, but now you are light in the Lord. Live as children of light for the fruit of the light consists in all goodness, righteousness and truth" (Ephesians 5:8). In verses 12–14, he goes on to say, "But everything exposed by the light becomes visible—and everything that is illuminated becomes a light. This is why it is said: 'Wake up, sleeper, rise from the dead, and Christ will shine on you.'" Finally, he says, "Husbands, love your wives, just as Christ loved the church and gave himself up for her" (Ephesians 5:25). The only way you can hope to truly love your wife as you ought is by walking in the light of Christ.

Perhaps at this point God has illuminated a dark room in your own life. Maybe you have no thoughts of lust in your mind. Maybe you are one who has already experienced the freedom that comes from fully walking in the light. If so, praise God! Be a light to those other men around you who have yet to find that victory. To the first man, the one who is now struggling in this area, I would say: don't wait another day in attacking this temptation. Don't even have the thought that it's not a problem. It is.

During our time together, I have intended not to point a finger or speak in an accusatory tone. Such methods are Satan's ways. I am very much aware of my own frailty, so every word that I have written in this book was first a word to myself. I am simply a desperate man seeking to help other desperate men and looking for those who will join me in the battle. We're stronger together!

Even as I was writing the devotions for my son and future daughter-in-law, which has become the basis of this book, I sensed the rousing of a defeated enemy. I knew full well that he wanted to defeat me before I even got started. He didn't want this word getting out that you can be free. When I sensed the enemy was on the move, I knew my only hope was to bring the battle to the *light*. I told my wife, as well as confessed to a brother in the Lord who prayed with me and for me, and my mind was renewed for the battle.

Satan uses his lies on every man to make him quit before he even gets going. You know the lies. You've heard them before: "It won't happen; you can't change; she won't believe you even if you try."

Did God bring you this far to leave you? Did He ignite the ember of hope in your heart just to extinguish the flames? What's the chance of that? No, God has brought you this far because He has a plan and a purpose and the power to fulfill the promise.

Today's couple activity will, perhaps for many, be the most challenging of all that we have done. As individuals and as a couple, I ask you to step out in faith and believe that the *truth* has set you free, that God through Christ has already forgiven you every sin, and that through the gift of forgiveness, each to the other, healing power is now flowing through your marriage.

Know that I and many others have prayed for those who have reached this point. Even now Jesus is praying for you and has given you a grace that is fully sufficient for this moment.

Couple Activity

As you prepare for this couple activity, keep in mind the following truths:

Therefore, if anyone is in Christ, the new creation has come: The old has gone, the new is here!
—2 Corinthians 5:17

Therefore, confess your sins to each other and pray for each other so that you may be healed. The prayer of a righteous person is powerful and effective.
—James 5:16

- Confess to each other those things that you have tried to keep hidden in the darkness.

- Wherever there is a remnant of the old lie still lurking, confess it now.
- In humility and awareness of your own sinfulness, forgive each other.
- Pray for each other, thanking God for the gift of your marriage and God's power to make it new.

Day 29

When the Stork Arrives

Discipline your children, and they will give you peace;
they will bring you the delights you desire.
—Proverbs 29:17

At one point in time, when our four boys ranged in age from one to seven, I really did have this insane idea that I could write a book on good parenting. How silly is that? If the age of realization for a man is twenty-seven, as it was in my case, then I am still waiting on the age of realization as a parent. If I can live long enough to see them all get their *AARP* cards, then maybe I'll write a book on parenting. For now, I shave my head (as I have done for the last fifteen years), because of all the bald patches where I was pulling my hair out. I guess that I'll continue this practice, since I still have a few more years to go before my parenting responsibilities are done!

I have to smile—I want to fall on the floor and laugh hysterically— when I hear a young parent say, "Little Johnny has hit those terrible twos." If every activity under the heavens has a season, you are going to love the activities in seasons thirteen through twenty-one. At two, they're just getting warmed up while they're wearing you out. I heard a theologian (or was it a comedian?) declare that "they have finally pinpointed how old Lucifer was when he rebelled against God and took a third of the angels with him; oddly enough, he was fifteen."

Parenting truly has been one of the greatest joys and challenges of my life. Sometimes you have to take a moment to laugh, because if you have been a parent for a while, you have probably already shed many tears—not all bad tears, but tears just the same. The day I pronounced my oldest son and his sweetheart husband and wife, the tears were there. When I saw him graduate from basic training to serve his country, tears were there. I have shed sweet tears at different times in each of my boys' lives—whether it was when Nathan, for the first time, shared a song he wrote; or when Chad made us laugh even while lying in a hospital bed; or when Tyler snuck up on his mom to give her a bouquet for Mother's Day. Along with the tears of joy have been those of anguish. The tears of awareness are the ones I cherish most—those tears that come when I see how God has blessed each boy with amazing wisdom as he has grown.

If we have grasped the principles of wisdom found in the book of Proverbs, then we understand that day never comes when our parenting responsibilities are done. Our responsibilities as parents will change over time, as will the relationship with each child, but they never fully go away. Your call as a parent is to live your life in such a way that your children will always consider you as one from whom they can always seek wisdom. If my dad were alive today, I would be seeking wisdom from him even at the age of fifty-two.

On day 28, we talked about the value and importance of both finding and being a mentor. Parents need mentoring too. I am always looking for insight from men when I can see that their children have blessed

143

them with peace as a parent. Sherry does the same with women. Hopefully the day will also come when the transformation of your responsibility as a parent moves you more into the role of being a mentor to your children than a provider. We do them no favors by continuing to provide for them when they are well on their way to adulthood. Neither will parents find peace in their lives by giving their children everything they want or failing to discipline them for their actions. Children need to understand the consequences of their actions. A parent will never have the privilege of mentoring an adult son or daughter in the wisdom of God if that child was raised with an entitlement mentality.

Not long ago I was in the local phone store getting a new phone. A girl, perhaps fifteen, was angry and disrespectful with her father because she wanted the latest smart phone that her friends had. The girl stormed out of the store screaming, "I hate you!" I watched the girl leave only to see the dad go ahead and buy his spoiled brat of a daughter a phone. Hebrews 12:11 states, "No discipline seems pleasant at the time, but painful. Later on, however, it produces a harvest of righteousness and peace for those who have been trained by it." Parents who refuse to discipline their children train them for something, but it's not righteousness and peace. We see the evidence of a lack of discipline throughout our society today. I don't blame parents for all the troubles of society, but I would say parents that fail to properly discipline their children greatly diminish the possibility of ever experiencing the joy and peace that can come from a healthy parent-child relationship.

Being a parent brings a sacred obligation to train up that child. You— not the school, the state, your neighbors, Grandma or Granddaddy— have the responsibility to train that child. Others will help and likely be glad to do so if you are training your child to produce a harvest of righteousness and peace, but they will also be quick to turn from that task if you are shirking your own responsibility in this arena. Proverbs 13:24 tells us that those who love their child are also careful to discipline that son or daughter. Failure to do so is negligence.

Not only is discipline a sacred obligation, but it is also an incredible honor and may just be our last hope as a nation! You are either helping to rear the next generation of freeloaders who will write the last chapter in our history books or that of warriors—men and women of God who know who they are in Christ and are unwavering in their identity and the knowledge of the truth that set people free. I truly believe we are that close. Things are happening in our nation that will overtake and destroy those who have no wisdom. I didn't point out all those verses of the Bible that foretell such, but they are there. Some things in life are more important than making sure little Johnny gets an iPod for Christmas. If you are already a parent, or are preparing for that day, give much thought and prayer to your responsibility in training that child to be one who knows and seeks wisdom over material things.

The three toughest questions I have ever been asked came from a man whose children were grown. He asked, "But what if you are an empty nester? What if the relationship with your kids is nonexistent? What encouragement do you have for me?" Trying to answer those questions reminded me of the idea I had that I could write a parenting book when my kids were all less than seven. I haven't ever experienced his situation and have been greatly blessed in my relationship with my sons, so I couldn't speak from personal experience. I know that perhaps some reading this book are brokenhearted over a severed relationship with a grown child. Perhaps all you can see in your life is a sad story of a lifetime of dysfunction, bitterness, and brokenness. My heart breaks for you as I struggle to find answers to your questions.

Though I am unable to speak from personal experience, I do hope that you will be encouraged. I have seen God's grace restore many broken relationships between parents and grown children. Change is possible. God can restore that which is broken. It will take faith on your part to believe that with "God all things are possible" (Matthew 19:26). God is not concerned with determining who was right or wrong but rather longs to generously give you the wisdom you need without finding fault, as described in James 1:5. In His eyes, the main thing that matters is the restoration of the relationship. With the saving grace of God at work in your life, you can be empowered to take steps of healing, to make things right. When grace is truly at work in your life, it will move you in ways that you never thought possible. Such a radical shift in your course can have extremely positive consequences in your family's life but will not automatically erase the negative effects of the relationships you were experiencing. The circumstances may not change at all, at least not immediately. The scars may remain, but healing can begin at the moment we begin to exercise our faith and move boldly forward.

The Prophet Joel prayed, "O God, redeem the years the locusts have eaten" (Joel 2:25). Perhaps you could have that same prayer. Before Jacob and Esau were reconciled, Jacob prayed for the Lord's mercy and favor. The Bible says he actually "wrestled with God" through all his hopes and fears (Genesis 32:28). He was very much aware of his own sin and knew that his only hope was mercy. As Jacob knew that he must have God with him to go before his brother, so must a parent who would seek to reconcile with a grown child rely upon God working through him or her to mend the broken relationship. Before he went to his brother, Jacob told God, "I will not let go of you." Jacob knew the greatest blessing in life is that of restored relationship.

Like Jacob, hold on to Jesus. You don't know what the outcome will be, but in your heart you know that you must do what you can to make things right. You humble yourself and put down every prideful thought. You give God all your fears and then do what God says do. *You go.* It may be painful. Jacob's hip was thrown out of socket as he wrestled with God. He wept and laid all his pain on the altar before God and then went to his brother, walking with a limp. God honors a broken and contrite heart.

Although I have an incredible relationship with my sons, I have been guilty at times of saying hateful words out of frustration or chastising them unmercifully for something they did. I have had to ask for their forgiveness. A father who is not willing to ask for forgiveness raises children who do not know how to give or ask it for themselves.

After twenty years without contact, Jacob and Esau were reunited with no laying of blame. Esau had been careless, while Jacob had been deceptive; however, those things no longer mattered. The brokenness was behind them—a lifetime behind them. All that mattered was reconciliation: "Esau ran to meet Jacob and embraced him; he threw his arms around his neck and kissed him. And they wept" (Genesis 33:4). Tears of forgiveness are more precious than gold. Jacob tried to give Esau his flocks and herds, but no demand of restitution had accompanied the mending of the relationship. When Jacob realized the free gift that Esau had given him in making no demands, he said the only thing he knew to say: "to see your face is like seeing the face of God" (Genesis 33:10).

In the eyes of God, forgiveness is the greatest gift that one can give to another. It is a reminder of the power of the cross and the price that was paid so that those who believe can experience the greatest gift of all. I have seen the face of God in my sons when I have asked for their forgiveness. I know many others who have experienced this gift from another. I also know many who want to. If you are one of them, I pray that you would find the reconciliation you long for and experience the joy that comes from the greatest gift of all.

Couple Activity

- Discuss how wisdom will guide you in the training of your child.
- How will such training produce peace and strengthen the parent-child relationship?
- What steps might you need to take now to reconcile a relationship with your children?

Day 30

It Takes Three

Every word of God is flawless;
He is a shield to those who take refuge in him.
—Proverbs 30:5

A few times over the years I have actually wanted to throw some couples out of my office. I never have, but *I have* thrown up my hands. "What are we doing here? First, neither one of you is going to use me to bolster your position. Second, I am *for* marriage. I'm for *this* marriage. Neither of you appears to be, though. You don't have one gentle answer between you—just a lot of 'he said; she said,' back and forth."

Proverbs 30 describes such a man as a brute without understanding and a woman who is so contemptible that the earth trembles that she even married. Harsh words, yes, but I have witnessed such marriages. "You've lost that loving feeling" is putting it lightly. Maybe you know couples like these. You may even identify with the Righteous Brothers song, because your loving feeling is gone. Hopefully such is not the case.

Since you have read this far, be assured that at least a small ember of hope is buried underneath all the pain, an ember that tells your heart that you *can* have a great marriage, even now. I can't imagine a man or woman reading even the first chapter in the absence of such hope; therefore, we will dispense with all this talk about "teeth like swords and jaws set with knives" as referred to in Proverbs 30:14. Such couples do exist, but I wouldn't expect them to read this book. Perhaps you have been in such a position at times in your life, but I am reminded of the apostle Paul's words to the Corinthians, "And that is what some of you were. But you were washed, you were sanctified, you were justified in the name of the Lord Jesus Christ and by the Spirit of our God" (1 Corinthians 6:11).

I do want to highlight the last five words of chapter 30 because sometimes Christian couples need this reminder even when they are committed to the principles of wisdom in building their marriage. The last verse says "stirring up anger produces strife." We already know these words to be true, but I wonder sometimes if couples are really aware of the things that stir up poisonous anger within the relationship.

How many times have you said, "You're just like your mother (or dad)," not intending the statement as a compliment. That question, by the way, is not the reason this chapter is entitled "It Takes Three," but for many couples it is the fastest way to stir up anger and produce strife. Maybe your dad is a brute or her mom is contemptible, and one of you has behaved in a fashion similar to the poor role model of a parent. Accusing your partner of being a mirror image of that parent is certainly not arguing according to the fair rules of engagement or the *think before you speak* principle we learned earlier on day 15. Bringing Mom into the picture is not fighting fairly. Brutes and contemptible couples use such strategies. If you are using them, stop. Enough said.

Whether you are a couple preparing for marriage or one that is trying to restore loving feelings; whether you have been working through *31 Days from Now* as a couple or reading as an individual, the bottom line is that a successful marriage takes three.

Perhaps your pastor asked you to read this book in preparation for your marriage. I want to speak frankly to you right now. If you are committed to a Christian marriage but have questions about your fiancée's commitment, please, please, please weigh heavily the words that I share now.

In Amos 3:3, the prophet raised the question, "Do two walk together unless they have agreed to do so?" This commitment is more than a spiritual matter; it is also a practical one. When you say "I do," don't you hope that the other "I do" will be from a person who loves the things you love and wants to engage in the same activities as you? I'm not talking about whether she will go to the gym with you. I've been trying to get Sherry to go to the gym for years. That activity is just not one she enjoys, at all; however, were she to feel the same about having a personal relationship with God, we would have a recipe for real trouble. You would be asking someone to be part of your life in a way that is unlike any other relationship, but that person has no interest in the most important person in your life. Does that really make sense, practically speaking?

The emotional feelings of love can make us do crazy things. We just feel extremely good to feel loved, but love is much more than a feeling. When the excitement of the chase has faded along with the feelings, you got what you got, but is it really what you wanted? Unfortunately many couples say no. The divorce courts are filled every day with mismatched couples because a believer was not willing to heed the wisdom of God's Word.

Our focus text today from Proverbs 30:5 states, "Every word of God is flawless; He is a shield to those who take refuge in Him." Before you say "I do," I beg you to please run to the refuge. Seek the wisdom of God. Don't be afraid to ask Him to reveal His will. Don't be afraid to consider the wisdom of godly parents and friends. Many times God uses others to reveal His will. My mother cried many prayers for me in those dating years. I consider it a miracle that I listened to her when she suggested that I might want to ask Sherry out. I have seen Sherry cry many prayers as well for our boys and have witnessed the answer to those prayers. Save yourself a world of grief; run to the refuge, and consider every letter of the flawless Word of God as you run.

Maybe you have been married for many years. Perhaps you have been reading this book because you and your partner have had problems. Maybe you were just looking for material to help your marriage be even better. Again, you probably would not be reading this sentence if you were not at least a spiritual person.

Jesus said in John 10:10, "I have come that they may have life, and have it to the full." His desire is for you to have a full and meaningful marriage that will bring you great joy all the days of your life. All the wisdom that we uncovered from Proverbs is the flawless Word of God. If we heed what it says, we can have the marriage we always wanted. The man who reads these words without the Spirit of God will see them as the mere words of men. They may be good words like any other book that might help in some way, but they are just the words of man. Without the Spirit, you won't see ways to implement many of the principles that Proverbs describes. You may even believe that many of the principles provided there are foolish. Again, the apostle Paul tells the Corinthians, "The person without the Spirit does not accept the things that come from the Spirit of God but considers them foolishness, and cannot understand them because they are discerned only through the Spirit" (1 Corinthians 2:14). No place is this more apparent than in the area of forgiveness. We find it difficult to offer forgiveness when we have not recognized our own need for it in the first place.

More than twenty years ago, after graduating from seminary, I was having my little "self-righteous" devotional time. Not all devotional times are self-righteous, but when we think we are making points with God, they are. God was about to show me so. Suddenly He spoke to my heart just one word: "David." The dialogue in my heart went something like this. "Okay, Lord, I will pray for David, our next-door neighbor who has just lost his son." Again God spoke the name David. "Okay, Lord, I will read the Psalms and all the stories of King David. I know he was a man after your heart, and I am too." Once again I heard that small voice, "David." My response, "Lord, I know what you want, but I can't do that. Besides, it was so many years ago. It was another place in a town far away. Besides, I don't know where David is now. Plus, he never knew it was me. Again, "David." At the time we didn't have Google and the ability to find people with the click of a mouse, so I got the big, thick Atlanta phone book and looked for David. To my utter surprise, he was living in the same town that I now lived in and was only three miles down the road. "Okay, Lord, I found him. I ask your forgiveness for what I did. Thank you for reminding me. I feel better now."

"David."

With trembling hand, I dialed his number, somewhat praying that no one would answer; however, on the third ring, he did. I immediately recognized his voice—a voice I had not heard in ten years since graduating from high school. We exchanged small talk for a few minutes, before I said, "David, I would like to stop by sometime and visit with you."

He said, "Well Ken, that would be great, but this is my last day in town. I am moving in the morning to Florida." Again the voice, "David."

I said, "Well then, I will come over now to see you off."

Ten minutes later, I was sitting on David's couch in a room full of packing boxes. Again, we exchanged small talk until I confessed. "David, do you remember the night the tires were slashed on your 442 Oldsmobile? That was me. I'm the one who did it." I reached in my pocket and pulled out my checkbook. With pen in hand, and too ashamed to look up at him, I said, "I am here today to repay you." A moment of silence occurred. "How much do I owe you?" Again, silence filled the air until I heard words that have both haunted and hounded me for more than twenty years:

"I forgive you."

"No, David, I can't let you do that."

"Ken, I forgive you!" He went on to say the cost had been covered. "You don't owe me anything."

I don't remember much about the conversation after that. In fact, I rather quickly made an exit, telling David, "Thank you; I'd better go to work now." Then, for the next twenty minutes I sat in my car and wept. Even now as I type, the tears flow down my cheeks. That day haunts me when I think that my stubborn self-righteous pride almost kept me from experiencing a blessed reminder of the heavenly Father's forgiveness. It was so close the whole time. It haunts me to think one more day of rebellion would have kept me from experiencing a deeper understanding of forgiveness. David showed me that day a reflection of the Father's grace and forgiveness that has inspired me to be gracious in forgiving others.

You're obviously a good person. After all, you spent the last thirty days considering the wisdom of Proverbs; however, the flawless Word of God reveals that as good as we think we are, it's not good enough in our own strength. God loves us so much that He gave us the free will to live our lives the way we want to. With that freedom comes the ability to choose between right and wrong. If you are honest, you have to admit that you've made the wrong choices at times; otherwise you probably wouldn't be reading this book. God calls all the wrong things we have done sin. Sin separated us from God, not because He was mad at us but because He is Holy God. The Bible tells us, "For the wages of sin is death, but the gift of God is eternal life in Christ Jesus our Lord" (Romans 6:23).

Just as a criminal goes to jail in order to pay his debt to society, so our debt of sin has to be paid. The good news is that it was paid more than two thousand years ago by Jesus. Romans 5:8 says, "But God demonstrates his own love for us in this: While we were still sinners, Christ died for us." Romans 10:9–10 says, "If you declare with your mouth, 'Jesus is Lord,' and believe in your heart that God raised Him from the dead, you will be saved. For it is with your heart that you believe and are justified, and it is with your mouth that you profess your faith and are saved."

Trusting in Jesus as Lord and savior is the most important decision you will ever make, the only way a person can truly be a man or woman of God. That decision opens the gates to eternal life and empowers you to be the person you are called to be in your marriage. That's the power of God's forgiveness. That's why a marriage takes three.

Couple Activity

- Take time to discuss the meaning of the most important decision you can ever make. Hint: It's not the "I do" on your wedding day.
- If you have never trusted in Jesus and asked Him to forgive your sins, would you be willing to do so now? If you have already accepted Christ, would you pray that He work through you to show your partner love, encouragement, and support on a daily basis?
- Pray together, and, with God's guidance, seek and foster ways to strengthen your love over time and to avoid behaviors that create strife in your relationship.

Day 31

Honor What You Have Found

She is worth far more than rubies.
—Proverbs 31:10

Odyssey Marine Exploration has accomplished some of the most successful deep-ocean expeditions in the world, resulting in the discovery of hundreds of shipwrecks. While working on their project *Black Swan*, they discovered a Colonial-era ship with more than six hundred thousand gold coins weighing more than seventeen tons, valued at half a billion dollars. Valuable finds from expeditions around the world have been displayed in exhibits and shown in documentaries for all to enjoy, yet, hundreds (maybe even thousands) of antiquity's lost treasures await discovery.

The last chapter of Proverbs gives us the sayings of King Lemuel, whose name means "belonging to God." Lemuel is likely a symbolic name for Solomon, the primary author of Proverbs. He states that the inspired words are " … an utterance his mother taught him" (Proverbs 31:1). If Lemuel is in fact Solomon, then the utterances are those of Bathsheba, who certainly knew a thing or two about the character of men. Married to Uriah, a man of noble character who fought valiantly for King David—a man of questionable character at the time—Bathsheba had no choice but to become the king's wife after he had her husband killed in battle. Is it not intriguing that as Bathsheba's first husband was a man of great honor, King David, through many trials and tribulations, become one himself? I would also note that, of all the words of wisdom that we have studied, the final thoughts of Proverbs are those of a woman. Would that we knew more, not only of her words to her son but to Uriah and David.

"Behind every good man there is a good woman." That's not a patronizing cliché. It's the truth. Because of her, he " … lacks nothing of value. She brings him good, not harm … She speaks with wisdom, and faithful instruction is on her tongue …" (Proverbs 31). The Odyssey has discovered incredible treasures, but a man who finds a good woman has found that which is worth far more.

Just as the Odyssey continues to search the seas, so too are you just beginning to realize the incredible treasure you have found and to realize you have even more to discover: her mind, her beauty, her love, her soul—a vast sea of yet largely unchartered waters. And perhaps the greatest treasure of all you have already discovered if you are married—she said "I do" to you! You make no mistake by investing the remainder of your days praising God for the gift that she is and the treasure you have found.

If you are just beginning this journey of marriage or are soon planning to do so, I want to congratulate you for completing this thirty-one-day journey with me. I pray that I have shared a few nuggets or so from my own experiences and the wisdom of Proverbs that will be of great benefit to you in the days ahead. I am greatly encouraged that you have read *31 Days from Now*, not so much for what I have shared, but because of what the great *book of wisdom* has to say. God's Word has greatly blessed my life. I hope that it has blessed you, as well. As you apply the principles of wisdom we have studied here, I am confident that God will bless your marriage, and that it will be more joyous than you ever dreamed.

If you have been married for some time, I want to commend you for continuing to press forward. Perhaps, like me, you have seen marriages all around you floundering and failing. Perhaps your own marriage has been in question and is so, even now. While no magic formula is available that will guarantee success, a mighty God is ever-ready to give you everything you need to strengthen all that is good about your marriage and restore that which is broken.

> Indeed, if you call out for insight
> and cry aloud for understanding,
> and if you look for it as for silver
> and search for it as for hidden treasure,
> then you will understand the fear of the Lord
> and find the knowledge of God.
> For the Lord gives wisdom;
> from his mouth come knowledge and understanding.
> —Proverbs 2:3–6

I pray even now that from this day forward, you will be captivated all the remaining days of your life with the mystery and majesty of your beloved. May your life's study be to know her ways, experience her love, appreciate her beauty, and benefit from her wisdom.

Couple Activity

In the next chapter, we will offer one final couple activity. Today's activity is your lifetime activity, one that will shape who you are and help you in implementing all other activities we have covered here, as well as those you will undertake as you progress on your spiritual journey.

- Her lifetime activity: How will you seek always to be a woman of noble character?
- His lifetime activity: How will you seek to be a man worthy of the treasure you have found?

The Final Chapter

Soldiers are dying all around me—not in the desert, but here on the home front, from the battle that continues to rage within their own hearts and minds. At twenty-two suicides every day, veterans account for a disproportional 20 percent of those who end their lives in our country. I'm no war hero, but I am often called upon to save those who are while serving in my role with the Armed Forces Mission and as a chaplain in the US Army.

I am equally concerned with saving military marriages and strengthening marriages for all people. According to the National Vital Statistics System, each year throughout the United States, more than one million marriages end in divorce. Many of those couples are my dear friends. Just as I stand with our soldiers, I must also stand with those who struggle to believe that God would have their marriages be so much more than they are now.

Most of us have been in situations where the only thing we could do was weep. When Sherry and I were rushing to the hospital as our third son, Chad, was being air lifted to the Grady Hospital Burn Center, we wept the entire way. When I stood by my dad's hospital bed in 1989, and a few years later my stepdad's hospital bed, I wept. In those times when I have buried soldiers as *Taps* began to play, tears streamed down my face. When I hear of friends struggling in their marriage, I have a deep ache in my heart. Perhaps you have wept many tears over your marriage. I am reminded that the shortest verse in the Bible is two words—"Jesus wept" (John 11:35).

Several years ago in my personal Bible reading, I read that Nehemiah also wept. He wept as he looked out over his homeland filled with destruction and despair. However, what really hit me was that he "wept before the Lord." At times in my life I have cried out to God, "*Why*? What is the point of all this pain? God, how can You be in control? Do You really love me? God, do You really care?" Looking back now, I have come to believe that many times weeping is an act of faith. The tears uncover that fertile ground of faith upon which the glory of God springs forth. The Psalmist wrote, "Those who go out weeping, carrying seed to sow, will return with songs of joy, carrying sheaves with them" (Psalm 126:6).

I don't know what is going on in your life, but I know that in the midst of your pain, your broken spirit, and all the grief you can bear, if you will cry out before the Lord, the Almighty God will hear and respond to the tears of your broken spirit.

I also saw in the Bible that Nehemiah came to the realization that God was calling him to a work he had never considered before. He was calling him beyond the pain and back to the promise. The day you said "I do," you no doubt made many promises, and you likely had no clue as to the work that would be involved in keeping those promises. A strong marriage does take work, but God's promises about marriage give us the strength we need to carry out our promises in the marriage relationship. God promises He will give us everything we need for that work. It is God's promise that makes a way for grace and forgiveness to transform our individual lives. It is His promise that allows grace and forgiveness to heal broken marriages and restore the love you once knew.

Maybe your thoughts toward your husband or wife are not good right now, but God's thoughts toward you are. He wants more for you than you have ever asked or imagined. He can restore that which is broken. Like Nehemiah and so many others, you are not bound to wallow in the mire of self-pity and brokenness forever; however, you do have to believe in His promises. He will give you the strength and wisdom to believe once again in the promises you made on your wedding day.

We have touched briefly in this book on the importance of forgiveness, but I am still not sure that many people grasp the idea. Who can, really? After all, it's an idea originating in the infinite mind of God. But every so often, God does give us glimpses of its power. While we may not fully comprehend forgiveness, we must accept that it is the essential key to restoration and healing.

I continue to stand in awe of the transforming power of forgiveness in those times when I have crushed Sherry with hurtful words. Her forgiveness has a way of humbling my prideful spirit and her love draws me back to the place of peace and harmony. If you say you can't do it, that you can't forgive, then you won't; however, it's about God's power, not your own. The mystery is that He often uses human beings to reveal and do His work, but you must be open to the idea that God desires to reveal such power through you. You will know that you have it when the air of self-righteous superiority is gone and what remains is a humble realization that the forgiveness you have shown is because of the forgiveness that God has shown you.

Something strange and wonderful happens when we allow the power of forgiveness to operate in our lives. The ember of hope that was smoldering under ashes of brokenness is fanned into flame. We come to know that God really is our only hope and that our joy is restored by wanting what He wants. God desires His glory to be revealed in you and through your marriage. Apart from the glory revealed in the cross or the glory revealed in the birth of a child, there is no greater place to reveal His glory than marriage. Is it little wonder why the battle rages so intensely against marriage in our day?

Logically we may tend to think that if God is our only hope, then we should just sit back, kick our shoes off and say, "Okay, God, You're in control." Rather than sitting back, however, the man or woman who has a passion for God's glory takes action. The ground that is yours is only yours when you take the step of faith. The waters of adversity roll back, and the opportunity is revealed when you move forward with a divine sense of purpose in mind. In the midst of the struggles and even the battle, God is calling you to action.

When Nehemiah took action, he was also taking a huge risk. He was a simple cup bearer for the king. Going before the king unannounced could have cost him his life. He didn't know if he would find favor or death, but he did it anyway. When he spoke to the people of Jerusalem about their broken condition, he could have been with them saying, "What's the use? We're ruined. It's over." Taking action always involves risk, whether it be in implementing a strategy on a battlefield in the desert or in deciding to fight for your marriage. Nehemiah's message to the people is with a sense of urgency. It is a rally cry to the people. He says to them, "Come and let us build the wall of Jerusalem, that we may no longer be a reproach." He is speaking to the pain in their lives, but he is pointing to the promise.

He gives them a purpose; he cast forth a vision—a better day is coming.

Not long ago, I spent two weeks at Fort Dix, New Jersey for Command General Staff College, learning the strategic and operational art of *Ends-Ways-Means* and strategies of war. It's a military concept that has application in our personal lives as well. The end-state that we seek in our personal lives is peace and stability. On the international scene, when diplomacy fails, the result is often war. In marriage, when efforts at peace fail, the result is often divorce or a lifetime of dodging emotional mortars between a brutish man and a contemptible woman.

The never-ending battles between husband and wife prevent the desired end-state of a joyful marriage. While war has often been described as simply a continuation of policy among nations, and even a means of economic recovery through the military industrial complex, it is hardly the best policy or "way" for couples to reach their objective. Nations have a certain resiliency that helps them recover from war, but family war can deteriorate relationships beyond recovery, and the desired end-state is lost forever.

I still vividly recall the emotional grenades that I tossed at Sherry in the early years of our marriage, when I was totally focused on where I wanted to spend the holidays without giving thought to her needs. To her credit, she was a very resilient woman who loved me in spite of my stupidity. Thankfully, in turning to God's Word for the wisdom I lacked, I discovered His "ways and means" for obtaining the marriage I truly desired. The book of Proverbs speaks of seeking to understand—of doing what is right, just, and fair. I still have much to learn, but I am encouraged that I can add to my learning through the wisdom it reveals.

When marriage conflict does arise—and it will—listen. Seek to understand, but in those times when you don't, then do what is right, just, and fair. You would also do well to keep your desired end-state in mind. What are you trying to achieve? Do you truly want to promote a positive environment? Do you want a relationship of love and acceptance that inspires the other and enhances positive growth and development of the relationship? If such is your desired end-state, then you must be very strategic and intentional in developing the ways and means that will achieve your desired goal. Peace never happens by wishing it were so. It will take work and more effort than you can possibly imagine at this moment, but the foundation you establish in the beginning or from this day forward will open the door to a blessing that you cannot fully comprehend. One day, you will, though!

The final lesson I learned from Nehemiah are the words he shared immediately following the declaration of the vision he had for a restored city: "The hand of my God has been good upon me." (Nehemiah 2:18) I will never forget that night with my sons as we stood in a country graveyard. Tyler was prepared for his Man Walk, and the time had come to show other men the desire of his heart. It was a tradition that had begun with my oldest son eight years earlier. Tyler was now the last of my sons to take this walk, following in the footsteps of MaCrae, Nathan, and Chad. It was an intensely emotional moment for me and each of the men there. We stood for some time talking about the men now laid to rest—the visions they had, the lives they had lived.

Before we left Tyler standing there alone, I pointed out the words inscribed in the stones, the final words of these men. Then I gave my sons instructions for the day they would stand there for me. When

I die, this shall be my final word: "The hand of my God has been good upon me." In the midst of the pain, the heartaches, the setbacks, the darts of despair, the hand of my God has been good upon me. In those times when I could have given up, given out, and rolled over, the hand of my God has been good upon me.

As we come to the final chapter of this book, I hope for a new beginning for you or a renewed sense of hope that with God's help and through His wisdom, your marriage can and will be what you dreamed when you said "I do."

I also told them about the
Gracious hand of my God on me
and what the king had said to me. They replied,
"Let us start rebuilding." So they began this good work.
—Nehemiah 2:18

Afterword

A Woman's Point of View

By Sherry Koon

Growing up with two sisters, a mom, and two female dogs, my dad often felt overwhelmed by the estrogen that filled our home. At certain times of the month, Dad would go fishing. The tables were turned when I became a wife and mother. A husband, four sons, and four male dogs increased the testosterone environment over 600 percent from what I was used to. I had a lot to learn. Guys are risk-takers, and it starts at an early age. One day we walked out on the back deck to find three-year-old Nathan climbing on the outside rails of the second-story balcony. Another time I walked into the kitchen to find two-year-old Chad swinging from the chandelier over the kitchen table. Multiple trips to the hospital, including one life flight, stitches, broken bones, and the totaling of several vehicles are just some of the many experiences that have challenged me over the years.

One evening at dinner, our oldest son who had just taken his first job seemed deep in thought. Ken asked him what was going on. MaCrae, who was fifteen at the time, shared that an older guy at work was challenging him. I was concerned that MaCrae was being bullied, and I said, "Well you just tell that bully to be sweet to you." All four boys including Ken began to laugh hysterically. "Are you kidding,

Mom?" MaCrae asked. Ken added, "No son, don't tell him that." He looked at me and said, "Honey, none of my boys are ever going to tell another man to be sweet to them. MaCrae, you have a black belt in karate. If he keeps it up, put him on the floor." I will say that Ken does not advocate violence, but he's not afraid to stand his ground either, and he has raised the boys to do the same. A lifetime of father-son retreats, a house full of guns, athletic trophies, black belts, and even a national power lifting title attest to the fact that Ken has done all he knew to do in raising the boys to be real men. In many ways I have felt like a spectator. It's one of the reasons I have prayed so much for the boys all their lives; not just that they would survive their growing-up years, but that one day they would marry young ladies with whom I could develop common interests.

While I may have different views from a house full of guys, the one area where Ken and I have had strong common agreement is in the subject of chapter 1 of this book: "To be a man of God is the most important thing." These really were the first words the boys learned. At the time, I don't think that Ken or I grasped what we had set in motion by making this the family credo for the men of the house. It has for both of us been an incredible challenge and at the same time a wonderful blessing to catch glimpses of how God has and is even now honoring that decision.

Over the course of writing this book, Ken came to me many times wanting to know my thoughts about each chapter. This is one area where I have seen personal growth on his part over the years. He has learned to appreciate my thoughts and opinions and even confided recently that I have helped him to understand what it means to be a man of God better than most men have, especially regarding husband-wife relationships. In his words, "A woman does a much better job teaching a man how to relate to a woman than a man does." I am glad he finally figured that one out. I am also glad that he finally understands that working through issues with your mate is totally different from dealing with a bully at work. When he is "sweet to me," he does get a very positive response.

Recently we were working through day 12, "The Power of Words." We began the couple activity, "Listen as she tells you about a time when your words felt more like a sword than love." I recounted a time on the little league field many years ago when he was coaching. We were down with no runs; the kids in the dugout were out of control; and parents in the stand were ridiculing the coaches. As the pitcher was warming up for the last inning of a shutout, Ken came to me to get some gum. I made a suggestion. Ken, in a loud, obnoxious voice for all to hear, shut me down. I recounted how his words had made me feel so small, how they felt like a knife in my spirit. I was embarrassed by his actions, and the rest of the season I lost interest in his coaching.

In accordance with the rules of the couple activity Ken actively listened without saying a word. He sincerely regretted that after all these years I still had a vivid recollection of that day, and he asked for my forgiveness. Then he asked me what he had done lately that made me feel small and insignificant. I shared with him that when we were at dinner a few nights ago, I was talking to our new daughter-in-law. It was a conversation that I thought all four of us were involved in, but instead of listening, he began a sidebar conversation with our son. It reminded me of that day on the field a dozen years ago. Thankfully we both agreed that it was time to reactivate Operation Woolly Booger.

I know Ken has not shared this with you, and I am a bit embarrassed to do so because of the name, but it works. Wooly Booger is a code between Ken and me for when we need to have a talk or settle an issue on a matter that could cause the other to be defensive.

In our day 12 couple activity, Ken shared that, "Men are always accused of being the ones who are defensive, but women can be just as defensive, and they can hold a grudge far longer than men."

I admit I don't like to hear the words, "We need to talk." Those words seem so serious to me, and they make my insides knot up. I also don't like the words, "Please don't get defensive about what I am about to say." That's like telling someone not to think about the color blue. What do you do? You think about the color blue. Thus, code words work best for us. Ours is "Wooly Booger." It's the same words I would use with the boys when they were toddlers. If they were doing something they shouldn't be doing, I would say, "Don't be a Wooly Booger." They knew stronger disciplinary measures were in store if they persisted.

When Ken and I use the phrase, we know that we need to talk about something that may be a little touchy. The code words help us prepare for a tough discussion or cease whatever activity it is that is causing the other person distress. It may also generate some strange looks from dinner guests, but what a great way to open a conversation with others that might be of benefit to them.

If I would add anything that was not specifically addressed by Ken, it is the importance of husbands and wives being united in encouraging each other to pursue their dreams, the ones they had before marriage. My dream was to be a stay-at-home mom. When

MaCrae was born, I left my job to pursue that dream with Ken's complete encouragement. Fulfilling the dream has been a challenge, but Ken knew going into the relationship that this was what I wanted to do. Ken was also up-front with me from the start that he desired to pursue his master's degree in North Carolina. Being a mama's girl, it was difficult to move four hundred miles away, but I knew Ken had a dream. Certainly the best marriages are the ones that understand the importance of willing sacrifice, but the greatest marriages are the ones where both partners encourage each other to pursue their dreams, not change them. If after marriage, I had demanded that we stay close to home or Ken had demanded I get a job to help pay the bills, we would not have the marriage we have today. Rather than a marriage filled with joy and contentment, there would no doubt be some, and perhaps much, resentment. For this reason, I highly encourage individuals to be up-front from the start in sharing their dreams with their potential significant other in their life. Compatible dreams, where each partner can see themselves as part of the other person's plans for life, provide much stronger footing for building a successful marriage, and it greatly reduces the likelihood of the "If you love me …" arguments. I am reminded of Martin Luther King's "I have a dream …" message, one of the most inspiring messages of our times. He had a dream, a vision, of where he wanted to go and what he wanted to do that captured many hearts and transformed a nation, as did Abram, Joseph, Jacob, Samuel, Uzziah, Ezekiel, Daniel, Amos, and Zechariah to name a few from the Bible. My encouragement to my boys and to all young people is to pursue your dream and trust that God is big enough to raise up the one who is willing to walk with you in the pursuit of yours, even as she pursues her own. In this way you are truly walking together. After all, "Can two walk together, except they be agreed?" (Amos 3:3).

Last evening, we had dinner with one of the couples that Ken spoke of on day 21. He was the man who bought the book Ken had recommended and was applying the principles. We had a wonderful time of fellowship, and things are much better for this couple, as he has taken to heart the challenge of being the man God has called him to be. Ken shared with them a strategy that he has used and shared with our sons. *One degree* of change can make a huge impact. I recall Ken sharing the concept of *one degree* with six hundred soldiers in basic training at Fort Benning.

Shooting for the moon once seemed an impossible task. But that is no longer true. However, we must be precise and clear on what we are seeking to accomplish. A space shuttle that is off by one degree will miss the moon by four thousand miles. One degree makes all the difference in the world. Hot water turns into boiling water because of one degree. Cold water turns into ice because of one degree, and a soldier who thinks one degree of immorality, disrespect, or laziness is no big deal will miss the prize.

When applied to marriage, it's not about taking and giving orders; it's not about legalism. Rather, one degree is all about relationship. Relationships, whether between spouses or friends, superiors or subordinates can be greatly improved by a willingness to adjust by one degree. A vision of one degree will empower a soldier to make it through basic training and husbands and wives to move back to a place of joy and love in marriage. In Ken's words,

> It's not brokenness that destroys a soldier but attempting to carry the broken pieces all alone. We are soldiers. We take care of our own. We never leave a fallen comrade, and we never quit. We will

show grace and understanding for the burdens of our fellow soldiers. As your chaplain, I will be an example of strength to others—not through spouting self-righteous, dictatorial platitudes but through the redeemed brokenness of my own life and the grace which makes it so.

I am blessed in my marriage, because my husband has allowed the brokenness of his own life to be a place where grace abounds. After twenty-nine years, our marriage is still a work-in-progress, and we both continue to grow in our understanding of all God intends it to be. We also recognize that having a great marriage is hard work and takes much prayer and commitment.

I pray you have benefited from the things Ken has shared and that your marriage will be one that brings great blessing to you and great glory to God.

Couple Activities

Somehow even in our technological age, writing things down seems to cause us to remember things better than electronic recordings. In the introduction I encouraged you to create a couple's journal or an individual journal. If you have not yet done so, here are the couple activities from throughout the book to help you to get started.

- Share your story with each other. What is your earliest memory? What inspired you? What was a challenge? What wisdom have you gained to this point?

Day 1

- What does it look like to be a man/woman of God?
- What part does grace play in your personal identity?
- What are the important (immutable) truths for your marriage?

Day 2

- What will discretion look like within your marriage?
- What relationship wisdom speaks to you in Proverbs 2?
- How will you seek to increase wisdom as a husband/wife?
- What insights that the other may have right now will you be willing to attend to and apply in your life?

Day 3

- What benefits can you imagine by exercising wisdom in regard to finances?
- What is your plan for paying off current debt?
- How will you seek to honor the Lord in your finances?

Day 4

- What acts of personal discipline will you incorporate for the benefit of your marriage?
- According to verse 4:7, how much is wisdom worth?
- What is meant by the words, "Give careful thought to the paths of your feet ..." (verse 4:26)?

Day 5

- What boundaries are you putting in place in regard to others outside your marriage that will protect you and your relationship with your spouse?

Day 6

- Begin thinking through your personal mission statement and your marriage mission statement. What would each of those include?

Day 7

- What does personal power mean to you?
- How does wisdom increase personal power?
- How will you use your personal power to build and strengthen each other?

Day 8

- How would she feel knowing she is your primary "go-to" person for insight and decisions?
- In what areas of your life will you begin to implement that commitment now?
- Make sure you have the signals right. Ask her to coach you through them. She'll be glad to; that's what great coaches do.

Day 9

- In what ways will you seek to display wisdom as you entertain others in your home?
- Describe a time when you were able to be a source of wisdom and encouragement to someone?
- What safeguards will you employ to guard against giving and receiving unwise invitations?

Day 10

- Share with each other something that the other has done that conveys love and meaning for you.
- Tell your spouse of at least one activity or task the other could engage in on a regular basis that you believe would benefit your home and/or relationship.

Day 11

- Express your commitment to each other that you will endeavor to always look for the good.
- What is one good thing about your partner for which you are, right now, thankful?

Day 12

Today's activity will be a challenge. Don't let it become a fight.

- Listen as she tells you about a time when your words felt more like a sword than love.
- How does wisdom guide your response?
- Listen as he tells you about a time when your words felt more like a sword than love.
- How does wisdom guide your response?

Day 13

- How will you work together to overcome the persuasive power of the illusion of success?
- Make it a high priority over the next few days to create a mutually agreed-upon budget.

Day 14

- Ask her how you can best demonstrate good will in your marriage. Don't make any promises; just work on building goodwill.
- Do you have a tendency to be quick-tempered, lazy, or indifferent? If so, how might these traits create problems?
- When the challenges come, how will "giving thought to your ways" guide you?

Day 15

- Share with each other some examples of times when the other has spoken compassionately and given encouragement in a difficult situation. Remember to repeat such words of encouragement and love whenever you get the opportunity. Express gratitude when your spouse does the same.

- Discuss and agree to some basic "rules of engagement" that will guide you through the challenging times.

Day 16

- In the past when you have been hurt or offended by your spouse, what has been your typical response?
- How will you seek to respond in the future when such times arise?
- Do you have one or more places of pain right now where the healing process can begin to take place though the act of genuinely forgiving your spouse?

Day 17

- Where is the finger of God touching your heart just now?
- How has God revealed His character to you in a time of testing?

Day 18

- Ask her to tell you what good communication looks like to her. What does it look like to you?
- What changes do you need to make now that will strengthen your skills at listening?

Day 19

- Ask her how you can demonstrate that you cherish her way of thinking.

- Ask her to point out one way that you can improve how you relate to others. Step out of your comfort zone, and be aware of how you can put into practice what she reveals.
- What will your life together look like when you get there—ten, twenty, or thirty years from now?

Day 20

- In what ways have you recognized your defensiveness when you and your partner disagree?
- Describe a time when you were more focused on the "me" rather than the "us" in your relationship.
- Brainstorm with your partner ways that you can show respect to each other during times of disagreement.

Note: Our goal is not to focus on past hurts, but hopefully after twenty days of working through the couple's activities, you understand the purpose of such exercises. We're looking for a little bit of self-reflection that can help spur personal growth and strengthen the relationship. It's not about one spouse reminding the other spouse of how defensive the other is, but it is about you recognizing within yourself those things that hinder the relationship so that you will be able to better navigate around such potholes in the future.

Day 21

- Share with your partner something good that he or she brings to the relationship, whether it be a consistently uplifting way of expressing love, a steadfast attention to keeping the household running smoothly, or some other gift. Think of ways you can continue to express your appreciation to your partner for the positive things he or she does in your daily lives.

- Till this point I have not asked you to pray together as a couple. Hopefully you have been doing so all along. Today's activity is to pray with each other, asking God to give you wisdom that will bless your marriage and the strength to follow through on some of those earlier activities that perhaps you were hesitant to consider.

Day 22

- In what ways has your heritage (name) been a blessing or a curse? How might you benefit from developing a good name? How will you seek to implement the Proverbs 22:9 verse in your marriage and faith community?
- Name some ways you have been blessed by giving. Reflect upon how God blesses you as you give with a joyful heart.

Day 23

- What does "enough" look like to you?
- Is your attitude "I earned it; I'll keep it" or "God gave it; I'll give it"?
- What do your answers to these questions reveal about your character and faith?
- What changes, if any do you need to make in your priorities and values in order to live a more peaceful, Christ-centered life?

Day 24

- Identify in your relationship what your real treasures are.

- How much value do you put on that treasure?
- What will you do to enhance the value of your treasure?
- What are the tangible benefits of valuing the true treasure?

Day 25

- Ask each other the following: What is the one thing you would like to hear from me that I believe about you?
- If you struggle in your answer, say it anyway, with all the sincerity you can muster.
- Anchor that thought in your heart and mind as if it is cold water for a weary soul. It will be a blessing to you as well.

Day 26

- How will you differentiate between the important (essential) arguments and those that are a matter of personal opinion?
- What are some ways that you and your spouse can guard your hearts against deceit?

Day 27

- Who do you consider a potential mentor in your life?
- What will you do to foster such a relationship?
- In what ways will you seek to pass on the lessons you learn to others?

Day 28

- Confess to each other those things that you have tried to keep hidden in the darkness.

- Wherever there is a remnant of the old lie still lurking, confess it now.
- In humility and awareness of your own sinfulness, forgive each other.
- Pray for each other, thanking God for the gift of your marriage and God's power to make it new.

Day 29

- Discuss how wisdom will guide you in the training of your child.
- How will such training produce peace and strengthen the parent-child relationship?
- What steps might you need to take now to reconcile a relationship with your children?

Day 30

- Take time to discuss the meaning of the most important decision you can ever make. Hint: it's not the "I do" on your wedding day.
- If you have never trusted in Jesus and asked Him to forgive you of your sins, would you be willing to do so now? If you have already accepted Christ, would you pray that He works through you to show your partner love, encouragement, and support on a daily basis?
- Pray together, and, with God's guidance, seek and foster ways to strengthen your love over time and to avoid behaviors that create strife in your relationship.

Day 31

- Her lifetime activity: How will you seek always to be a woman of noble character?
- His lifetime activity: How will you seek to be a man worthy of the treasure you have found?

The Final Chapter

- If you have not yet developed your marriage mission statement, do so now. You should have a fairly good understanding of what it will include.

Our Marriage Mission Statement

_____

_____

_____

_____

_____

_____

_____

_____

_____

_____

_____

_____

_____

_____

_____

_____

_____

_____

_____

_____

_____

_____

_____

Name_____

Date_____

About the Author

Kenneth Koon is first a husband, second a father, and third a military chaplain. Sherry and Ken have been married since 1986 and have four sons. They have one very sweet daughter-in-law and are praying that one day they will have three more.

Originally commissioned into the US Army Reserves in 1991, Ken returned to service in 2010. Since that time, he has trained more than twenty-five thousand soldiers in spiritual reliance and suicide intervention and has been the keynote speaker at various commands throughout the United States. In addition to his primary work in intervention, he was trained at West Point through the Center of Army Professional Ethics as a master ethics trainer.

Ken is founder and Executive Director of Armed Forces Mission and AFM's Master Resilience Institute, an organization providing chaplain support and intervention services for troops and veterans. The institute provided continuing education training for more than twelve hundred mental health professionals, nurses, and law enforcement personnel in its first year and continues to expand its outreach. Ken also has a heart for training individuals from all walks of life in suicide intervention. Learn more at www. iwillintervene.com.

Ken is a graduate of North Georgia College, Southeastern Baptist Theological Seminary, and the Master's School of Divinity. Sherry and Ken make their home in Sharpsburg, Georgia.

About Armed Forces Mission

Founded Veteran's Day 2012
"We Build Resilience."

Our Vision—Through personal intervention for those in crisis and delivery of AFM programs and workshops, we are building stronger communities where individuals and families are finding the encouragement to face the challenges of life with the resources to adapt and heal.

What others are saying:

"One of the most intense (in a very emotional and moving way) environments that I have experienced in a long time."
—Scott Gilbert, Fayetteville, Georgia

"Rare people who really know how to connect with people ... high level of compassion and caring for others. I am grateful to work with such kind and compassionate professionals."
—Dr. Paul Wade, Army suicide prevention program manager

"A heart for Soldiers that extends beyond the Soldiers ..."
—Colonel John W. Aarsen, USAR

"A voice for the needs of Soldiers in the civilian community."

—Chaplain (LTC) Tim Bonner, USAR

"A high quality of performance ... articulate, caring, and sensitive ... most commendable."

—Colonel Tracy L. Dawkins, USAR

"An extraordinary way of reaching people ... overwhelmingly touched ... already planning the next event!"

—Major Connie Gonzales, suicide prevention officer, USAR

Visit www.StandWithThem.com to learn more!

Start a 31 Days Project

31 Days Project is an exciting new initiative of AFM's Master Resilience Institute to prepare couples for marriage and strengthen those who are already married. Both military and civilian couples will benefit from the four-week, small-group encounters based on the relationship wisdom from the book of Proverbs and Ken's book, *31 Days from Now.*

Contact us today to learn more about how you can start a 31 Days Project for couples or men in your church or community group. Visit www.31DaysFromNow.com.

Helpful Resources

The following books have been a tremendous blessing in our marriage and family life over the years.

Our Top List
the Holy Bible
Love & Respect by Dr. Emerson Eggerichs
His Needs, Her Needs by Willard F. Harley Jr.
The Five Love Languages by Gary Chapman
Bringing Up Boys by Dr. James Dobson

Sherry's Top List
The Power of a Praying Wife by Stormie Omartian
The Power of a Praying Parent by Stormie Omartian

Ken's Top List
Man in the Mirror by Patrick M. Morley
Every Man's Battle by Stephen Arterburn
The Love Dare by Alex and Stephen Kendrick
My Utmost for His Highest by Oswald Chambers
Good Husband, Great Marriage by Robert Mark Alter
Better Dads, Stronger Sons by Rick Johnson
Wild at Heart by John Eldredge
Half Time by Bob Buford
Wealth: Is It Worth It? by Truett Cathy

Printed in the United States
By Bookmasters